In the Footsteps of Orpheus

R. F. PAGET

In the Footsteps
of Orpheus

The story of the finding and identification
of the lost entrance to Hades,
the Oracle of the Dead,
the River Styx and
the Infernal Regions of the Greeks

*Illustrated with maps,
plans and photographs*

ROBERT HALE · LONDON

PRINTED IN GREAT BRITAIN BY
NORTHUMBERLAND PRESS LIMITED
GATESHEAD

Contents

Illustrations

MAPS AND PLANS

All photographs, with the exception of "The Source of the River Styx" were taken by the author. Maps and plans were drawn by T. R. Allen.

I dedicate this story to my wife
ADA IMMACOLATA
who for fifty years
has endured my idiosyncrasies
and encouraged my ambitions

Foreword

by the President, International Archaeological Society
(Allied Forces Southern Europe)

I first met Robert Paget in Naples in 1963, when he asked me if he could address a meeting of the Archaeological Society. On our way to the meeting, he told me of his interest in archaeology and of his researches in the local area. I was deeply impressed by his knowledge of ancient Baiae.

Later that evening we listened spellbound as he told us of his great discovery. With courtesy but with incredulity, we heard out his claim that he had discovered at Baiae the physical evidence of what all the world had hitherto regarded as poetic fantasy. According to Dr. Paget, Mythology had become reality. The concordance of his discovery with the references in the ancient writers was the most impressive part of his claim. At the conclusion of his speech Dr. Paget invited members of the Council to visit the site and see for themselves.

The reactions of members to Dr. Paget's statement ranged up and down the scale of human emotions. One was heard to remark "absolute rubbish". But the wiser and more shrewd members preferred to wait and withhold comment until they had seen and analysed the evidence for themselves.

A few days later, members in parties of five under the guidance of Dr. Paget made the three-hundred-yard journey underground. Even on the surface, in spite of conversions, it was still possible to trace the general plan of the Sanctuary of the Oracle, but underground the marvellous state of preservation of the tunnels, enabled every stage of the ritual to be envisaged.

We saw the Sixth Book of the *Aeneid* come to life before our eyes. Every important item, "The Dividing of the Ways", even to the cardinals that operated the Gate of Ivory, the Entrance to Tartarus, the River Styx, that "fount of potable

11

water" (Strabo), and the Sanctuary "far beneath the earth" (Ephorus) can be identified.

There is no doubt whatsoever in my mind that here, in Baiae, by Avernus where the "Cimmerians held the land in lease", we made the ancient pilgrimage to the Realm of Hades.

I am fully aware of the great importance of this discovery and the need for caution in accepting a claim of this magnitude. There are, however, too many items of proof to be mere coincidence.

The aspect of the main entrance passage with the enormous number of lamp niches, clearly indicates a ceremonial usage. The co-ordinated efforts at suppression and blockage of the tunnels with conversion of the surface buildings to other uses, all indicate that here was the Cult of the dead that Agrippa had done so much to eradicate.

The confirmation of the existence of this Oracle, will stimulate renewed interest in the history of the Phlegrean Fields, especially of Baiae itself. Who knows what secrets still lie hidden under the vineyards. Here Julius Caesar had his summer palace. Cicero lived at Pozzuoli and Horace wrote "Baiae. . . . No place in the whole world can rival your glorious Bay". Here a hundred thousand slaves toiled through their miserable lives, comforted only by the thoughts of eternal life promised them by the Oracle of the Dead and later by the New Religion emerging in the Near East.

This great archaeological discovery by Robert Paget, formerly of the Royal Navy, and by Keith Jones of the United States Navy, has already been described by the Italian Press as the pearl of the twentieth century.

It is a magnificent example of Anglo-American co-operation, working together to help unravel the hidden mysteries and culture of this great and ancient host nation of Italy. It would not have been possible but for the enlightened policy of the Italian Authorities of encouraging amateur archaeology which is being so splendidly implemented, and with so much international goodwill, by the very learned archaeologist Professor Alfonso di Francisis, the Superintendent of Antiquities for the Campania, under whose overall supervision the members of the International Archaeological Society in Southern Italy operate.

In recognition of his outstanding contribution to the cause of archaeology in Southern Italy, the Council of the International Archaeological Society (Allied Forces Southern Europe) has elevated Dr. Paget to the dignity of Honorary Fellow of the Society.

Naples   J. C. Gates
January, 1964   Squadron Leader, R.A.F.
                                                      PRESIDENT

Introduction

What this Book is about

This is a book about Orpheus and the Underworld. The phrase is reminiscent of comic opera and can-can music. Orpheus is imagined as a legendary figure, serving only as an inspiration for poets and musicians.

These conceptions are wrong, Orpheus was one of the greatest thinkers who has ever lived. His name has been a household word for millenia, yet all that the average man knows of him is the legend of his descent into the Underworld in search of his wife Eurydice.

In fact, he was a religious reformer comparable with Buddha or Mohammed. He prepared the Grecian world for the reception of Christianity and he had a great deal of influence on its concepts. His religious tenets were so similar to those of Christianity, that in the first and second centuries A.D. all the thunder of the early Christian Fathers was brought to bear on them, to suppress them and his name.

It was he who first developed the concept of a 'soul', and the judgement after death of the righteous and the evil-doer. His concepts still form the basis of the Christian Purgatory.

This is not comic opera. It is fascinating human drama and this is what this book is about.

This is the story of the discovery and identification of the Great Antrum at Baiae near Avernus, which the Ancients believed to be the Entrance to the Underworld, with its mysterious underground Sanctuary, where initiation took place into the Cult of the Gods of the Infernal Regions.

The site was buried in the landslide following the great earthquake in A.D. 63 and its very existence forgotten. Although it had been visited by Hannibal, and Vergil had based his story of the visit of Aeneas to the Underworld on his personal knowledge of the site (he lived at nearby Lucrino), modern students had come to believe the whole thing to be nothing more than a poetic fantasy invented by Homer and Vergil.

In 1960 I came to live at Baia and found myself surrounded on every side by the ruins of past Greek and Roman glory. Then I met Keith Jones, and what was intended to be a mild excursion into archaeology between the intervals of sunbathing and *dolce far nientë*, became the commencement of a new life of research and delving into the past to satisfy a desire to know more about the way people lived around the Bay of Naples, 2000 years ago.

We had to re-learn our school Latin and Greek and plunge into the maze of Greek Mythology. We spent days and weeks in the National Library in Naples and in the Museum of Antiquities.

It was not long before we became fascinated with the legends and beliefs in the Underworld, Life after Death, and Gods of the Infernal Regions—all centred round the crater of Avernus. We remembered the phrase *"Facilis descensus Averni"* (the way to hell is easy) and were surprised to find that Vergil had written this more than 2,000 years ago. Did he know the way to the Underworld? We found that Strabo, Ephorus, Livy, Pausanias, Silus Italicus and many others of the old writers all spoke of these things as physical facts—they believed the legends to be true. What is more the site was at or near the Crater of Avernus. We determined to find out if any traces remained of the temples and sacred places.

One hundred years ago, the retired German business man Heinrich Schliemann was considering a similar problem. At that time everyone believed that the city of Troy was a figment of the imagination, even that Homer himself had never really existed. Schliemann preferred to believe Pausanias and the other ancient writers and dug up the city of Troy under the Hill of Hissarlik at the entrance to the Dardanelles. Inspired by Schliemann's success we believed that Homer, Ephorus and Strabo, Livy and Vergil all knew of the physical existence of the Oracle of the Dead and when they said it was near Avernus, this was a fact. It was burial by the landslide that had caused the fall into oblivion.

In order to gather our evidence we visited all the archaeological sites within a hundred miles of Naples. We soon learned that 'Comparison' is the secret of archaeology. A style of architecture, a type of masonry, or wall decoration at one place is the standard, when the date is known, with which to compare a local discovery. Pottery found at a site or in a tomb, is used by excavators all the world over to date their finds. Even a small piece of broken pot is sufficient in many cases especially in the Campania to identify the very distinctive types that were made at the various known centres, and exported all over the Mediterranean.

This book cannot begin to tell of the hours of study, or recapture the countless disappointments in the field. Where to begin our search, was the first problem. This we solved by deciding to start at Cuma, and if necessary enter and explore every hole in the ground in the Phlegrean Fields.

How many did we enter? We have lost count, it must have been many more than a hundred. Some were damp and smelly, some dry and smelly, but all more or less charged with sulphurous and other volcanic gases, the homes of scorpions, poisonous snakes and huge black spiders with bodies as big as nuts and legs three inches long, barring the way with their sticky webs and poisonous bites . . . fitting guardians to the Gates of Hell.

But there was a tremendous fascination in our search. Ruins and other traces of Roman, Greek and Stone Age men, show themselves in almost every field. The curious rise and fall of the sea-level due to the aftermath of the formation of the Mediterranean Basin in Tertiary geological times, demonstrates that Italy and the Aegean area still float freely on a molten mass of lava very close to the surface, the pulsations in which, due to changes of pressure, cause the changes in level. These changes have left Circe's Island, Cuma and Cape Misenum high and dry surrounded by wide flat plains where formerly they were islands and the plains, pestiferous malarial marshes.

Then the craters, eighty-seven of them in a radius of five miles from Avernus, give the surface of the land as depicted on a map the appearance of a congealed glue-pot. And this is exactly the case, the sea entering cracks in the rocks found the molten lava. Immediately there is a tremendous explosion due to the sudden conversion of the water into steam. The surface

B

rocks were blown to dust, just like a bursting bubble and the surrounding countryside was covered with the dust to form the great beds of tufa building stone which today form the hills of the Phlegrean Fields. At the junction of the walls and floors of most of these craters are hot water springs and gas fumaroles to tell us that the fires are still smouldering and ready to burst out again at any moment. Only twelve years ago, there was a sudden incursion of boiling water into Lake Lucrino (adjacent to Avernus) which killed all the fish. In 1538 a great mountain 450 feet high was thrown up in forty-eight hours, right in the middle of Lake Lucrino.

There is so much sulphur in the air that all our silverware goes black and it is necessary to keep it in plastic bags.

Yet this volcanic earth of the Campania is so fertile that it produces four crops a year, under the vines that cover the terraced hill sides in every direction. And it has been equally fertile for more than two thousand years. This is what Strabo says, writing in 50 B.C.: "As proof of the fruitfulness of the country, it produces the finest grain, I mean the wheat from which groats are made, which is superior, not only to every kind of rice, but to almost all other kinds of grain food. It is reported that in the course of only one year, some of the plains are seeded twice with spelt, the third time with millet and others still a fourth time with vegetables, and it is from here that the Romans get their famous wine the Falernian."

With the coming of the Pax Romana about 150 B.C. the transfer of Greek culture to the Roman youth began to take place in the schools of Naples and the Phlegrean Fields. It became the most intellectually populated region of the world. All the philosophers, all merchants, all theologians, even all spies and revolutionaries, all came to Puteoli and Baiae in their due time.

Here was the meeting point of all the religions of the ancient world. The time was ripe for a vast new religious concept. The ancient religions were in a decline and their influence fading. The Romans had made the hopeless experiment of trying to replace them by deifying the State in the person of their Caesars. How did they expect such a 'god' to offer the consolations of religion to subjugated peoples, when it was a constant reminder of their servitude. So they came from Palestine, from Asia Minor and Alexandria to meet at Puteoli and Baiae to discuss the merging of many cults and religions into the infant Christianity.

Vergil clearly indicates that Orphism was practised at the Oracle at Baiae. I have devoted a chapter to a description of Orpheus and his beliefs as I feel most people know little about him.

There is little doubt that the Great Antrum was used for different purposes at stages in its long history. Written evidence is extremely scant and the history of the Cuma/Baiae areas during the last five hundred years B.C. is very difficult to reconstruct. There is considerable doubt as to when, in fact, the Great Antrum at Baiae was closed—or did it just fall into decay? There seems to be evidence for a Senatorial Decree about 186 B.C. entitled "De Bacchanalibus" which was directed against the abuses of these processions. This may also have affected the Antrum and caused closure of the Oracle if Dionisiac initiations were practised there. All these matters are still actively being studied by the author. As so often happens with a discovery of this nature, new lines of research are opened up. In this book I have accepted the date of about 37 B.C. as the date of closure by Admiral Agrippa. Readers will appreciate that I made this decision with the reservations described above.

The discovery was made during 1962, the first entry being on September 21st. As soon as the proofs were consolidated, we reported the details of our discovery to the Superintendent of Antiquities for the Campania, who kindly granted us permission to continue our researches at Baiae. The announcement of the discovery was made to the Press on November 22nd, 1963, who immediately hailed it as the "gem of archaeological discovery in Italy of the twentieth century". Since that date, as we have learned more about it, the importance of the discovery has greatly increased. There is now no doubt that here at the Great Antrum with its underground Sanctuary, was a religious centre of pilgrimage and reverence that endured for many centuries. We hope today it will endure for many more as a source of study and inspiration to the modern world. The mystery of the old cults still pervades the long tunnels and to conclude this introduction I would like to quote a letter I had from a friend I took down to the Inner Sanctuary of the Oracle. This is the letter from Colonel Edward J. Voso of the United States Army. "My sincere thanks for permitting me your company to the Underworld. My reactions to the visit were of mixed emotions; initially it was one of simple curiosity which increased in intensity due to your infectious enthusiasm, then finally to a feeling of guilt for being within the confines of a place held Holy by the Cimmerians. It would not have surprised me to hear the voice of the Sibyl echo through the tunnels . . . 'You are trespassing on hallowed ground. . . . Away, Blasphemers, to the surface.' I can truly say this has been an experience that I shall remember from now until my final journey across the River Styx."

R.F.P.

Bacoli,
Italy,
1966

Acknowledgements

We wish to express our grateful thanks to those, without whose generous help and encouragement, the whole enterprise would have been impossible:

Professor Alfonso di Francisis, Superintendent of Antiquities for the Campania,

Mr. J. B. Ward Perkins, C.B.E., Director of the British School in Rome,

Mr. M. W. Frederiksen, M.A., Fellow of Worcester College, Oxford,

Mr. Colin Hardie, M.A., Fellow of Magdalen College, Oxford,

Squadron Leader J. C. Gates, R.A.F., President of the International Archaeological Society, AFSE,

Signor S. di Steffano, supervisor of excavations, Baiae,

Guido d'Aiuto, Chief Custodian at Baiae,

Antonio Camerotti, Custodian at Baiae,

Vincenzo Scortino, Custodian at Baiae,

and the many other friends who helped at various times. A special thanks to Colonel David Lewis, U.S. Army, for his spectacular dive into the River Styx to help complete our survey.

We acknowledge with grateful thanks permission to quote from the following works, and we recommend their study to all those who wish to know more about these matters:

The Aeneid, trans. W. F. Jackson Knight. Penguin Classics
The Iliad, trans. E. V. Rieu. Penguin Classics
The Odyssey, trans. E. V. Rieu. Penguin Classics
Suetonius, trans. Robert Graves. Penguin Classics
Tacitus, trans. Michael Grant. Penguin Classics

The Greek Myths, trans. Robert Graves. Penguin Classics
Orpheus and the Greek Religion, W. K. C. Guthrie. Methuen and Co. Ltd.
Pausanias, trans. W. H. S. Jones. Loeb Library
Strabo, trans. H. L. Jones. Loeb Library
The Phlegrean Fields, A. Maiuri. Italian Government
Paestum, P. C. Sestieri. Italian Government

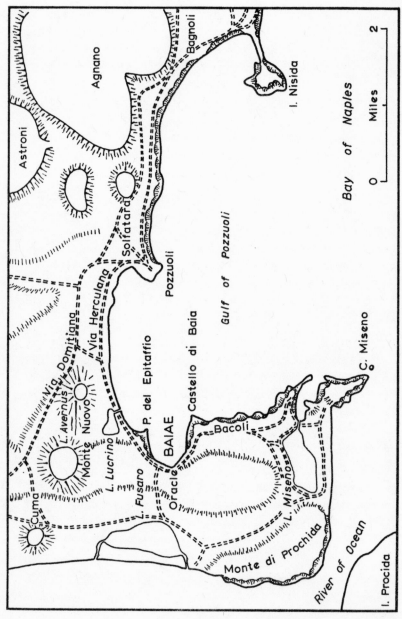

Fig. 1. THE PHLEGREAN FIELDS

1

The Phlegrean Fields

A few miles north-west of Naples lies that strange region called the Phlegrean Fields. It begins at Cuma, twenty miles to the north-west and ends against the ridge of the Vomero which forms the western boundary of the City of Naples. It extends inland for a maximum of five miles. Yet within this small area there are no less than eighty-seven large and small volcanic craters. The saucerlike depressions remind one of congealed bubbles, that have burst on top of a boiling gluepot. And this is just what did happen. The floors of the craters in all cases are practically at sea-level. It seems that the water coming in contact with the molten lava lying just below the surface, immediately became steam and the explosion blew the top off the bubble. The dust was deposited all over the Bay of Naples to form the beds of tufa building stone, in such demand today.

Winter is the best time to see the outlines of the craters, and to seek traces of Roman walls and Greek temples. The fertility of the soil is so great, that once the Spring sunshine has arrived, the vines and garden crops hide every inch of ground. Today there are no forests; all the hillsides are cultivated, by hardworking *contadini*, using no machines, but working all by hand, with only mattocks as tools. Such is the fertility of the ground that the task is accomplished four times a year. Peas, artichokes, maize, lettuce and many other varieties of heavy crops grow underneath the vines. And then in the autumn, anything up to one hundred pounds of grapes are gathered from each vine. The farmhouses probably occupy the same sites that they covered centuries ago. They make a delightful pink and white interlude amongst the greenery. The visitor's approach is

25

heralded by the barking of several dogs, the loud braying of a couple of donkeys loaded with faggots of sticks in panniers, and the inevitable rush of half a dozen dirty, but extremely happy small children. Country hospitality is a sacred duty and the visitor is invited to take a glass of their own home-made wine and harsh cheese made from sheep's milk, or if he is lucky, some curded buffalo milk that they call *mozzarella*. Visiting thus with the farmers round Baiae, where I live, the conversation soon turned on the traces everywhere of Roman times. Almost at every field there are jagged footings of old walls, or perhaps a coin has been found during the digging. One and all the *contadini* said none of them would work in the fields after dark, as there are too many earth-spirits abroad. The subsoil is so full of volcanic gas that little spurts of sulphurous anhydride cause bursts of flame visible after dark, and puffs of white smoke in the daytime.

The coastline is even more beautiful than the countryside. The wonderful sweep of the sandy beach, nearly sixty miles long from Circe's Headland at Gaeta to Cuma, the sequence of volcanic islands of Ischia and Prochida, and the long peninsula of Bacoli with Cape Miseno at its end which forms the north-western arm of the Bay of Naples itself. Along these hilltops in former times, the Roman patricians had their villas and the Caesars their palaces. Each bay is a small crater, and in many of them springs of sulphuretted hydrogen and boiling water testify to the fires beneath. The main street of Bacoli has been repaved three times since the Second World War, due to subsidence on a very unstable soil.

In the shallow waters of the Gulf of Pozzuoli, all along the dyke separating Lake Lucrino from the sea, can still be seen the paved streets, mosaic floors of the houses, even walls of the palaces and debris of winejars, broken pots . . . all that is left of Roman Baiae, the most luxurious sink of iniquity and riotous debauchery that the world has ever seen. Horace, the old reprobate Roman poet, lived here with his friends, Propertius and Vergil. He loved the pleasures of Baiae and writes, "Ah Baiae, no place in the whole world can compare with your glorious Bay."[1] On the other hand his friend Martial[2] lost his girl friend and complains "Baiae, grave of true love. . . . She came a Penelope, but returned a Helen." Today electric trains and motorbuses run along the ancient Via Herculana, past the frowning Monte Nuovo, past the Lake of Lucrino, where in 1955 a sudden incursion of boiling water killed all the fish.

All these things force us to think of the legends and myths that have been left us by the ancients, about this fiery region. Let us see what it was like in the time of Homer, one thousand years before our era.

We are able to reconstruct the scene fairly accurately, thanks to some very interesting researches carried out quite recently by A. W. Gunther throughout the whole length of the west coast of Italy.[3] He has been studying the changes in sea level that have taken place over the centuries, and has established that there has been a rhythmic rise and fall, like the pulsations of breathing, caused by changes of pressure in the molten lava masses on which the peninsula of Italy and the Aegean area simply float. The period of Emergence and Submergence is measured in centuries and the changes in level, at times, as much as 65 feet in many places. Indeed, he goes so far as to suggest that the submergence of the fertile coastal areas in the fourth century A.D. and the consequent loss of the greater part of the agricultural land of Italy, was one of the major causes of the general collapse of the whole Empire. This phenomenon is so prevalent, that it will appear constantly throughout our story.

Probably the most satisfactory way to get a general picture of the appearance of the Phlegrean Fields today is to take a bus in Naples, and make the trip to Monte di Prochida and Cuma. Here is a short description of the journey.

After traversing Naples and passing along the sea front of Santa Lucia and Chiaia, the route passes under the ridge of the Vomero through a tunnel, whose entrance is very near to Vergil's tomb. We pass out into the first of the great craters of the Phlegrean Fields, that of Bagnoli, on the floor of which is situated a fine modern steelworks which produces two million tons a year. From this hive of industry, the road gradually climbs up on to the top of the west wall of the crater, to a height of some 500 feet. To our left we look down the steep slope on to the sea, with the whole panorama of the coastline from Cape Posillipo to Cape Miseno in our view. On the horizon lies the island of Capri, shimmering in the haze. The Greeks called the Bay of Naples "The Gulf of Cuma", but the Romans gave it the significant name of "The Crater". On our right, we also look down to within ten feet of sea-level into the enormous crater of Agnano, no less than five miles in diameter, with boiling water springs at the site of the Thermal Spa originally built by the Romans, where today, two thousand years later, the baths are still hot. Looking ahead and still on our right, we can see that the west wall of the crater of Agnano is bright yellow with sulphur and smoking at many points. Here it is also the east wall of the crater of Solfatara, which heralds itself to our noses by the smell of its fires. Although Solfatara has not erupted within human memory, it is still a dormant volcano, liable to blow up at any moment. A walk across the crater floor is quite frightening, as every footstep testifies to the thinness of the crust upon which we are venturing; and all around are pools of boiling mud and blowholes of sulphur.

We are now in Pozzuoli, a concentrated conglomeration of six and seven storied apartment houses separated by the narrowest of streets, hung with the gaily coloured laundry of the occupants. Here are two great Roman amphitheatres, and the remains of the Roman port moles and quays. It is hard to believe today, but in 100 B.C. Puteoli was "The greatest port in the whole world".

As we are dealing with three different epochs—Greek, Roman and present day—I have followed the principle of using the place name appropriate to the epoch. For instance Pozzuoli of today was known to the Romans as Puteoli, and to the Greeks as Dichearchia. I think the reader will find no difficulty with the system which will help remind him of the times with which he is dealing.

Here, we are at the dividing of the roads, one of which goes north to Rome through the Arco Felice, built by Domitian to celebrate the completion, in A.D. 100, of the great Via Domitiana from Minturnae (at the junction with the Via Appia from Rome) to Cuma and Puteoli.[4] The other road, which is the Via Herculana and the one that we shall take, follows the dyke separating Lake Lucrino from the sea. In the fork of the two roads, lies Monte Nuovo, a volcano 450 feet high, thrown up in the course of two terrible days in 1538. Prior to this Lake Lucrino extended from Pozzuoli to Baia and inland as far as Monte Barbaro, say, almost two miles square. Two miles further on, we see the open gap in the eastern wall of the crater of Avernus, but the description of the crater lake must wait until later. The road now rises off the dyke to round the end of the Punta del'Epitaffio, into Baia. All along the cliff face are the entrances to cave-houses still inhabited. These dwellings are tunnels cut into the still hot hillside, and in the sea at the foot of the cliff below the road, a bubbling spring of hot water reminds us again of the fires beneath. At the very end of the Punta are the crumbling brick walls of the Temple of Venus Lucrina. As we round the point, we see across the Bay of Baia, the Castello di Baia, the grim Spanish fortress built by Don Pedro of Toledo in the sixteenth century, upon the south point of the bay and on the ruins of Julius Caesar's palace. In front of us is the steep wall of the crater forming the Bay, lined with terraced ruins of shops, houses and temples, the town of ancient Baiae, excavated in 1956. I shall say no more of Baiae at present as it is the centre of our researches. We see the road to Cuma passing over the ridge on the right, and it has cut into countless walls and tunnels of the old town, which in 100 B.C., possessed something like 25,000 inhabitants, against the mere two thousand of today. The busy little port of Baia forms a refuge for all kinds of craft in the sudden storms typical of the region. One vessel that is quite common is the felucca, a single masted coastal craft of about 60 to 80 tons burthen, which is exactly like the Arab dhow of the Red Sea and the *liburna*, or light scouting craft of the Roman navy, which Pliny says was copied from the fast Greek pirate ships operating out of the Albanian ports.[5] These ships are about 100 feet long by 15 feet beam; they could well have been copied from the fifty-oared galleys, that Homer says were the Greek warships at Troy. So here at Baia we can even see ships that link us with the navies of the Bronze Age.

As we climb past the Castello, we see a great tufa quarry on the right, from which building stone for the cities of the Campania has been dug for thousands of years. Practically nothing is left of Julius Caesar's palace—just a wall footing in the vineyard. But there still remains quite a lot of the first villa, built by the consul, Cneius Cornelius in 178 B.C.,[6] who came here to cure his arthritis with the healing warm waters. At the entrance to Bacoli, just beyond the Castello, and above the beach, are the ruins of a great villa, said by some to have been that of Pompey the Great. It even had a little private theatre, down on the beach. This is erroneously called by the locals "The tomb of Agrippina" (the mother of Nero, whom he murdered).

Here we are in a different world. Bacoli and Misenum were the site of the great Roman naval base. Each little cove was the scene of special operations; all are connected by tunnels driven through the headlands, to facilitate loading and unloading, and the provisioning of the warships. The port of Misenum consists of a fine harbour, which was connected with the inner lake of Misenum (Mare Morto), by a canal with a swing bridge. The outlet from the lake still uses the Roman canal today. All round the shores of the lake were barracks for the sailors, and tombs have been found giving the names of officers and even the ships in which they served.

But a thousand years before the Romans' time, the effects of the bradyseism to which I have referred, made the scene very different. The sea level had risen ten feet, or more, and the extra water in the channel between the island of Prochida and the mainland, caused a scour which removed the dyke of sand dunes now forming the sea barrier of Lake Misenum. A wide bay was then in existence, the extent of which can be traced by the levels on the map, and Cape Misenum was an island. When Odysseus came to consult the Seer, Teiresias, in the Underworld at Baiae, he beached his ship here in this bay, just where the track still called the Via Herculana comes down to sea level. In fact, this is right under my study window and in the half light, it does not require much imagination to bridge the 3,000 years and succumb to the temptation to look out and see if the ship is still there.

Skirting the Lake of Misenum, the Via Herculana runs behind the Monte di Prochida to Lake Fusaro before climbing to the Acropolis at Cuma. The ancients called Lake Fusaro, the Marsh of Acherusia[7] and considered it one of the exits of the Rivers of Hell. There is still a hot spring, about halfway along the lakeside which was said to be the outlet of the River Acheron in Hades. From there to Cuma is only about a mile. The hill tops are covered with vines and gardens; there are no longer any woods, or forests, or open grazing anywhere.

Before concluding my picture of today's scene, there remains to describe Lake Avernus. To get into the crater, there is a road that begins at the Cumana Railway Station of Lucrino. In a few hundred yards, the breach in the crater wall on the east side is reached. The time to visit it is on a calm summer's evening when the full moon is rising. There is a restaurant on the west side of the lake at the entrance to the tunnel of Cocceius (leading to Cuma), where you should dine on the terrace, right at the lakeside. You are looking out at a great circular mirror of dark brown water over half a mile in diameter. A black horseshoe of forest-clad cliffs over 500 feet high, forms the south, west and north sides of the mirror. But in front of you the east wall has disappeared, and the gap is filled with the dark menacing cone of Monte Nuovo. The full moon casts a ghostly light over the scene and a lane of whiteness on the waters of the lake. There is no wind to remove the ever present smell of sulphur; a dog howls in the darkness and you shiver with the sudden knowledge that you are in the Entrance to the Underworld, right in the Gates of Hell.

There are two dates of special interest to my story: namely 1000 B.C. or the time of Homer, and then the commencement of our era. These are first the approximate date of the voyage of Odysseus, and the second, when Vergil was writing the *Aeneid*. In Odysseus' day the hills were all covered with thick forests of poplar and oak. The first explorers sailing along the coast would have seen muddy plains intersected by narrow streams, and overgrown with jungle of bamboo and reeds. In the forests long trailing fronds of lichen hanging from the branches; and thick undergrowth hid wolves, bears and wild boar. Over all there were clouds of steam and sulphurous vapours from volcanoes far more active than they are today. The great mountain called Eponomeo, on the Island of Ischia (or Pithecussae, as the Greeks called it), was in a constant state of eruption until 500 B.C. The geysers and hot springs of the Bay of Baiae must have been like those of Roturua in New Zealand, or the Yellowstone National Park in the U.S.A. today. So steamy and hot was the air that Homer called it 'The City of Perpetual Mist'.[8] Solfatara, so far as can be judged, was in the same condition as it is today. The crater of Avernus even then, was well known all over the Mediterranean as one of the principal entrances to the Infernal Regions. How it came to be so considered, seems to show that its appearance must have been different from today's. Vergil's description speaks of "a deep and rugged cave, stupendous and yawning wide, protected by a lake of black water and the gloomy forest". Over this lake no bird could fly without harm in the poisonous gas that "streamed up from the black jaws and rose to the vault of heaven". I think there may have been a small island in the lake upon which was a crater puffing out carbonic acid gas and this island later disappeared, either in an earthquake or during the eruption of Monte Nuovo. Other than this, it must have been the strange mystery of the dark brown placid lake and poisonous atmosphere that intrigued those old explorers.

Homer's description of the coming of Odysseus is given at the beginning of the *Odyssey*, Book XI. It is as follows:

Our ship brought us to the deep flowing River of Ocean and the frontiers of the world, where the fog-bound Cimmerians live in the City of Perpetual Mist. When the bright Sun climbs the sky and puts the stars to flight, no ray from him can penetrate to them, nor can he see them as he drops from heaven and sinks once more to earth. For dreadful Night has spread her mantle over the heads of that *unhappy* folk.[9]

There is no evidence to show if there were any habitations at Baia or at Avernus at that far off time, but Cuma was already occupied by a Stone Age people who have left their graves on the north side of the acropolis.[10] Recent discoveries have found similar people at Paestum, about 60 miles south of Naples, whose pottery and other evidence dates them around 2500 B.C.[11] It was these neolithic men, who probably came from North Africa and spread over the whole of the eastern Mediterranean Basin, who first conceived the idea that chasms, caves and caverns in Mother Earth led to the Underworld and where these emitted mephitic vapours they established oracles. In the beginning all the oracles belonged to the Great Goddess of the Earth, but with the coming of the Olympic Gods (*see* Chapter II) Apollo took over custody of all the important ones, including that at Baiae. There is an important example of this at Cuma, where the Oracle of the Sibyl is of very ancient date. The temple above her Grotto is said to be dedicated to Apollo.

yet that it was founded and built by Daedalus, an Athenian in the employ of King Minos. In Roman times the temple was still in use and the statues and friezes made by Daedalus, showing scenes of life in Knossos in Crete, were common knowledge. Now according to Herodotus, the famous Greek historian, King Minos imprisoned Daedalus and his son Icarus, in the labyrinth, which Daedalus, himself, had built. Daedalus invented wings of wax with which they succeeded in escaping from the maze. Daedalus got free, but Icarus fell into the sea, as his wings melted in the heat of the sun. Some say however that Daedalus was the first to invent sails for ships and with these, they were able, easily to outsail the oared galleys of Minos.[12] Even so Icarus lost his life, as he was such a poor steersman, he capsized his ship. My reason for introducing this little anecdote, is that Herodotus puts the date of these events at "during the third generation before the Trojan War", say about 1300 B.C., a date which seems to agree reasonably well with the facts. Daedalus was a citizen of Minoan Crete and surely he would not have dedicated his Temple to Apollo at that time, but to the Earth Goddess.[13]

One of the great fascinations of archaeology, is that the evidence upon which many of the deductions are made is scrappy, to say the least of it. A piece of broken pot, a fragment of human cranium, the date on a coin—ten professors will give ten different interpretations, and each swear that his is the only possible version. I have had quite an experience of this in the last five years, and I now have no hesitation in putting forward my own hypotheses, based upon scanty evidence, if they seem likely to provide a starting point from which to work. Most of the deductions in weighty volumes, derived from the fragmentary evidence of pre-history, are little better than intelligent guesswork, however much they may be wrapped up in learned jargon.

Vergil wrote about the journey to Italy of his hero, Aeneas, the reputed founder of the Latin nation, after the sack of Troy. In his great poem the *Aeneid*, he says that the voyage of Aeneas took place only three months after that of Odysseus. When Aeneas arrived at the Island of the Cyclops, he found one of Odysseus' crew, named Archaemenides, who had been marooned when they blinded the Cyclops and escaped from

C

the island. Archaemenides says, "for the third time now the Moon is filling her horns with light, and for so long have I been dragging out my days in the woods and the wilderness, where only beasts have their haunts and lairs".[14] So it must be borne in mind at all times, that although the two stories were written a thousand years apart, they were contemporary. This is of special interest, because Homer got his information from explorers, of whom Odysseus may have been one, or Odysseus may be the comprehensive type, who brought the information to Homer at his home on the coast of Asia Minor. Vergil, on the other hand, lived at Lucrino with Horace and wrote an eye-witness account. The Oracle was undoubtedly there and functioning all through that thousand year interval of time. When Vergil lived here the hills were still covered with impenetrable forests and not even the Roman High Admiral dared to cut them down for timber for ship-building. The Cumaean Sibyl was the Mistress of the Forests and together with the priests of the Temple of Apollo at Cuma, exercised full control over the rites at the Oracle at Baiae.

Before we leave Odysseus, one last geographical note: Book X of the *Odyssey* says,

"But tell me Circe, who is to guide me on the way?, No one has ever sailed a black ship into Hell." "Odysseus," the goddess answered me, "don't think of lingering on shore for a pilot, set up your mast, spread the white sail and sit down in the ship. The North Wind will blow her on her way, and when she has brought you across the River of Ocean, you will come to a wild coast and Persephone's Grove, where the tall poplars grow and the willows that so quickly shed their seeds. Beach your boat here by Ocean's swirling stream and march on into Hades' Kingdom of Decay. There the Flaming River and the River of Lamentation, which are branches of the River Styx, unite round a pinnacle of rock, to pour their thundering streams into Acheron. This is the spot, My Lord, that I bid you seek out."[15]

Note that there is no mention of Cuma, although he must have sailed right past it, Circe's Headland being at the northern end of the long sandy beach which ends there. To me, the answer is plain. Cuma three months later welcomed Aeneas, so it must have had a Trojan population, as is maintained by the Greek historian Ephorus. It was therefore very unlikely that a wily old bird like Odysseus, being a Greek, would venture into such a trap.

Between Homer and Vergil the gap of a thousand years had brought great changes to the Phlegrean Fields. Cuma ideally situated from a defence point of view, on a small isolated hill, surrounded by marshes of impenetrable reed jungle, continued to develop as a naval power, doubtless making full use of the long peninsula of Bacoli-Misenum and its harbours. Cuma continued to colonise the Bay of Naples working round by Pozzuoli, then known as Dichearchia, and so to Naples, Herculaneum and the other towns on the littoral of Vesuvius—remembering, of course, that there was no 'Vesuvius' until A.D. 79 when the great eruption took place. Speaking of earlier times Strabo says, "Above these places lies Mount Vesuvius, which save for its summit, has dwellings all round on farmlands that are absolutely beautiful. As for the summit, a considerable part of it is flat, but all of it is unfruitful, and looks ash-coloured; and it shows pore-like cavities in masses of rock, that are soot coloured on the surface, these masses of rock looking as though they had been eaten out by fire. Hence one might infer that in earlier times, this district was on fire and had had craters of fire, and then because the fuel gave out was quenched. Perhaps, too, this is the cause of the fruitfulness round the mountain; just as at Catana it is said, that part of the country which had been covered with ash dust, from the hot ashes carried up into the air by the fires of Aetna, made the land suited to the vine."[16] Pompeii was an independent Samnite town, which traded with the Greeks entering the Bay of Naples from the southeast.

Cuma, which the Greeks called Kyme, and the Romans Cumae, was one of the oldest of the Greek colonies in Italy. It was first settled by Stone Age men who left their graves on the north side of the acropolis. The general view is that Italy was peopled originally by migrants from North Africa, known as Lybians, who came over into Sicily and Southern Italy some time between 3500 and 2500 B.C. Their largest settlement in the Bay of Naples area was at Paestum, where they left an extensive necropolis at a little village called Gaudo. Pottery and anthropological evidence tell us that these people were there in 2500 B.C. They were a maritime folk living on sea-food. Now sailors have a habit of being also explorers, so it would not have taken these people long to make the hundred miles north to Cuma. It can be confidently asserted that this is what happened.

There is much speculation as to where the first Greek settlers at Cuma had come from. Dionysius of Halicarnassus and Strabo say that the colony from Chalcis and Eretria, already established on the Island of Ischia (Pithecussae) were directed to Cuma by a dove sent by Apollo. Vergil borrowed this idea in his story of the *Aeneid*. Other sources, in particular Ephorus, say the founders came from Kyme in Asia Minor. I think Ephorus was possibly correct, when one considers that the voyage of Odysseus is now considered to have taken place. It was because the inhabitants of Cuma were kinsmen of the Trojans that Odysseus did not visit there. Also Ephorus is considered a reliable writer, and he was, moreover, a native of Kyme. Eusibus states Cuma was founded about 1050 B.C., which seems a reasonable approximation.

The argument that A. Maiuri puts forward in the *Phlegrean Fields* is, "It seems doubtful that, as affirmed by Strabo, Cuma could be the oldest Greek colony of Magna Grecia; indeed it is generally admitted that the foundation of Cuma should be attributed to the eighth century B.C. not before the foundation of Syracuse, and not before the establishment of other Chalcis colonies had opened up the Straits of Messina." In my view this argument does not appreciate the navigational problems of the Straits of Messina. Here were those awesome monsters Scylla and Charybdis, which Odysseus braved on his homeward journey. Homer and the Greeks knew of the tides, but of course they were not able to predict the times of high and low water as we can today. There difference of height at spring tides is a couple of feet or so in the Mediterranean. The tidal wave travels from Gibraltar to the Levant, and in its progress meets the barriers of Italy and Sicily, with only the narrow sea between Africa and Sicily and the Straits of Messina, by which to pass. The Straits of Messina are a funnel-shaped bight leading to a very narrow opening at the western end. The result is that for a small sailing-, or oared-vessel, the Straits are only passable at around high and low water. At all other times, the narrows are a turbulent swirl of whirlpools and tidal streams. For the same reasons the passage from the west is easier than that from the east and that is why Odysseus faced it on his homeward journey, not, be it noted on the outward journey, when he followed the recognised safe route, doubtless already well known, round Sicily. In any event to a ship coming from the Adriatic bound for the west coast of Italy, the lost time is not more than a day's sail under favourable conditions. Scylla and Charybdis must have prevented sailing through the Straits many years after the time of Odysseus. This effectively disposes of the argument that the colonisation of the west coast of Italy had to wait for the opening up of the Straits by local settlements.

There is a very extensive necropolis at Cuma. The discovery of a tholos tomb (i.e. a bottle-shaped tomb), points to the presense of Myceneans or Cretans. This alone indicates a date prior to 1400 B.C. when Knossos was destroyed. Inscriptions show that the Chalchidinian alphabet was first introduced here and spread to the Italiote tribes.

How was it that Cuma was founded before any other town round the Bay of Naples, especially along the Vesuvian littoral? Here again is a navigational explanation which may well suit the case. The first explorer from Greece, be it Odysseus or another, would naturally have sailed or rowed his ship northwards along the coast of the Bay of Salerno, then along the south side of the Sorrento Peninsula. When he reached the end, he found a hard north-east wind blowing with a heavy sea. He could not continue round the coast of the Sorrento Peninsula into the head wind and sea. But right in front of him only four miles away was the Island of Capri. He sailed across, and waited at Marina Piccolo on the south side for the wind to veer. He could now see Cape Misenum only twelve miles away to the north, whereas all he could see of the coast of the Bay of Naples was misty mountains twenty miles away. He took the fair wind and came to Misenum and Cuma. For years afterwards, all sea-captains would have followed the same route that had been pioneered by the explorer and known to be safe. Remember there were Sirens, Scylla and Charybdis and other unknown terrors. It is the duty of a sea-captain to navigate safely and not risk his ship in uncharted waters. So they all followed the first explorer across to Misenum. This is the reason why the military power of Cuma proceeded round the Bay of Naples from the north to the east, at least as far as Naples, whilst Pompeii and the towns adjacent remained independent in the hands of the Samnites.

Confirmation of this argument of mine has recently been provided by Col. David Lewis who is carrying out much underwater research in the Bay of Naples. He found no fewer than twenty-seven anchors from Greek and Roman ships all concentrated in one spot among the small Galli Islands, the home of the Sirens, which the old sea-captains had used as anchorage whilst sheltering from just such a north-easter as I postulated above. The anchors were lost through getting foul of the coral reef. When the crew tried to free them the rope cables broke and the anchors were in too deep water to be recovered. Lewis and I think this is a fascinating discovery of the ancient skill in seamanship, not risking their vessels in heavy weather. Some of the anchors would be suitable for vessels of fifteen hundred to two thousand tons burthen. They were doubtless engaged in the wine trade.

So far I have only mentioned the Stone Age pioneers. We know little about the period between 2500 B.C. and about 1200 B.C. when the Greeks began to come in numbers as refugees from the constant new waves of invaders in their homeland. Sometime in the eighth or seventh centuries B.C. the Etruscans came from somewhere, probably from Asia Minor, and settled most of Italy to the north of Rome. Greeks of various city-states occupied the coastal areas to the south of Rome both on the Adriatic and the Tyrrhenian side, whilst in the central mountain ranges of the Apennines fierce and hardy mountaineer tribes of Samnites, Ausonians and Lucanians established themselves. For the next three hundred years these peoples were at constant war with each other. At last the Etruscans gained power over the west of Italy as far south as the River Sele at Paestum. But their rule was mainly good only on the coastal plains. The foothills all along the eastern border of the Campania were still held by the Samnites. Lower down in Calabria, the Greeks never succeeded in dislodging the Lucanians. Then the Romans came on the scene and by about 150 B.C. they had succeeded in imposing the Pax Romana on the whole of Italy. For the first time there were stable peaceful conditions, in which the Greek culture and religion could be passed on to the Roman youth by Greek philosophers in the University of Naples and the Schools of Rome.

Cultural life began to concentrate on the Phlegrean Fields. I refer again to Strabo, who tells us:

> Neapolis has springs and bathing establishments that are not inferior to those of Baiae, although it is far short of Baiae in the number of inhabitants, for at Baiae, where palace on palace has been built one after the other, a new city has arisen not inferior to Dichearchia. And greater vogue is given to the Greek mode of life at Neapolis, by the people who withdraw thither from Rome for the sake of rest—I mean the class who have made their livelihood by training the young, or still others who, because of old age or infirmity long to live in relaxation; and some of the Romans too, taking delight in this way of living and observing the great number of men and women of the same culture as themselves sojourning there, gladly fall in love with the place and make it their permanent home.[17]

Such is the general picture of the whole Phlegrean region, with Cuma as the military capital, Pozzuoli the trading port, and Baiae with Avernus as the religious centre.

Pozzuoli was then called Dichearchia. As usual there was an acropolis which rises on an almost detached knob of lava, that at some time in the remote past flowed out of Solfatara. Continuing inland from the acropolis, there is a narrow valley between the crater walls through which, a very ancient road, the Via Campana, connects Pozzuoli with another very ancient track, later paved by the Romans and named the Via Appia. The Via Appia runs along the base of the foothills from Rome to Salerno, and then over the Apennine Range to Taranto and Brindisi. Down these roads to Puteoli came the trade of the Etruscans and the Samnites for export to all the countries of the Mediterranean, especially to the Aegean and the Near East. Strabo mentions olive oil from Venafrum, wines from Falernum, grain, rice and millet. The great market of Puteoli has survived in part to this day.[18] It was here in fact, that the phenomenon of bradyseism was first discovered. There were merchants from Egypt, Syria, Palestine, the Black Sea, the Aegean islands, Spain and Africa. So many that by 100 B.C. "Puteoli was the greatest port in the whole world". Very little official excavation has been carried out at Pozzuoli, so there are many untold secrets in many languages yet to be found. The great amphitheatre is the third largest in Italy, being exceeded only by the Coliseum in Rome and that at Capua, the provincial capital in former times. This great amphitheatre was built out of municipal funds and could seat 40,000 people. This is ample testimony to the immense prosperity of Puteoli at the height of its glory in the reign of Augustus. The slope of the hill was covered with the villas of the rich Levantine and Syrian merchants. The harbour was full of great ships, and I *mean* great ships, of two or three thousand tons. Cargoes of silk, ivory, timber, carpets, animals for the circus, passengers of all the nations of the east—all entered here on their way to Rome. St. Paul came here in A.D. 59 and the Acts of the Apostles tell us that he found believers in the New Religion here.

Legends about the Phlegrean Fields are based upon the conflict between neolithic 'Chthonic' gods, or gods of the soil, and the Olympic gods brought to Greece by the Achaeans about 1600 B.C.

Typhon, a fearsome monster who from the thighs downwards was a mass of coiled serpents whose mouths flashed fire and spewed out molten rock, was the god of volcanoes and dared to challenge the might of Zeus. He even succeeded in capturing Zeus and mutilating his fingers. But Zeus was rescued by Cadmus and blasted Typhon with his thunderbolt, throwing him down the crater of Eponomeo on the Island of Ischia. There he is to this day and every crater in the Phlegrean Fields is a mouth of one of his serpent legs. Another revolt against the Olympic Gods was that of the Titans, Lords of the Earthquakes and Rulers over the Planets. For ten long years the battle raged, until finally Zeus again intervened, and blasted the Titans down to deepest Erebus, the most terrible region of Hell, where they are confined to this day. The springs of boiling water and the geysers of steam and foul gas are the poisonous discharges from their fearful wounds received in the war.[19]

But the central legend was that of Avernus. This is the belief that here was one of the principal entrances to the Infernal Regions, that man originally came from Mother Earth and so to Mother Earth he returns when he dies. The etymology of the name Avernus is generally taken to be that it is a latinised form of the Greek *Aornon* (no birds), an allusion to the poisonous vapours from the crater killing the birds flying over. Robert Graves however, suggests another derivation from the Aryan root *Abol* meaning 'apple'. The first inhabitants of Greece were the Pelasgians (people from the sea), and in their myths they associated the apple with death. In the early days the various tribes were a totem society, like many of the South Sea Islanders in the Pacific today. They also had a matrilineal society. This means that the woman not the man was the head of the family. The reason was that the biology of fatherhood was not understood and it was the magic of woman herself, who produced everything. In the annual rites connected with rain-making and fertility in the fields, the High Priestess of the Goddess chose a sacred king-lover for the ensuing year. This entailed the killing of his predecessor by the new king. In the rites the priestess gave an apple to the old king as a death warrant and he was then ritually murdered by his successor in a variety of different ways according to the different totems. Another of the tabus imposed by totem society, was that the young men had to go outside their own totem to a related group for their wives. It was never the other way round, the women remained in the group and the men migrated. Perhaps the reason for this was, that it was an effective way of preventing any one family rising to too great power.

The life of man was compared with the daily journey of the Sun. At dawn the Sun mounts his chariot with its four white horses and commences his journey over the Earth. He sees everything that goes on and reports to Zeus all matters of interest. As he falls towards Earth in the west, and reaches the horizon, he unharnesses his horses, and descends from his chariot to pass the night in the Underworld before commencing his journey in the east again the next day. His horses graze near the garden of the Hesperides, where the tree grows that bears the Golden Apples. These apples were coloured green, pink, yellow, and red gold, the colours of the changing sky at sunset. As sunset occurs when the sun is half on the horizon, the evening star Hesperus appears. If an apple is cut across horizontally, it will be seen that the five-pointed star of Hesperus is always there in the apple. Some say that the apple was really a pomegranate with its blood red juice and many seeds. Statues of Isis, Hera, Persephone and even the Virgin Mary, represent the Goddess seated on a throne, holding the Child in one arm and with the other hand offering a pomegranate, at once the symbol of death and resurrection. This is the mystery of the cult of Avernus and the Underworld. Ever since Stone Age man first began to think on these things, the greatest religious minds have been directed to the problem. Yet we are no nearer to its solution today than were the men of old.

What was in the Underworld? It consisted of several regions each ruled over by a different overlord. The Realm of Hades with his Queen Persephone was bounded on the west by the River Styx, the other regions being bounded by its tributaries, Acheron (the River of Woe), Phlegethon (the River of Fire), Cocytus (the River of Lamentation) and Lethe (the River of Forgetfulness). The name of the Kingdom of Hades was Tartarus. The first region that the Shade of the Dead entered was the Meadow of Asphodel, a cheerless arid region, where the shades flutter about aimlessly, their only relief being the libations of blood poured in their memory by their relatives. Unless they had been provided with the necessary fee of an obolus, a small coin placed under the tongue of the corpse for its trip across the River Styx in Charon's coracle, they were doomed to remain in the Meadow of Asphodel for ever. Beyond this Meadow lies the palace of Hades surrounded by a grove of white cypress on the left concealing the Water of the fountain of Forgetfulness and on the right by a grove of white poplars, surrounding the Pool of Memory. Near this spot the Shades are judged for the Good and Evil they have done during their lives, by three stern judges appointed by Zeus, Rhadamanthus judges Asiatics and Aeacus tries the Europeans, whilst the difficult cases are referred to Minos. The place of judgement is where three roads meet, and according to the verdict the Shade is directed to return to the Meadow of Asphodel if neither good nor Evil, to the punishment hall of Tartarus if wicked, and forward to Elysium if truly virtuous.

Elysium is ruled over by Cronos (Time). It lies very near to the Kingdom of Hades, but does not belong to him. Further west still are the Fortunate Islands, reserved for those who have been thrice reborn on Earth and thrice attained Elysium. We shall learn more about Elysium when dealing with the subject of Orphism.

When Charon ferried the Shade across the River Styx, it was greeted on the far bank by the great three-headed dog Cerberus. "When he growls in all his three throats, the mountains tremble and the sound rumbles through the caverns of Hell." Cerberus greeted all newcomers by wagging his tail and pricking his ears, but he was ready to tear in pieces any who tried to return to the upper world.

The only way that one not already dead could enter the Underworld was with the help of the Sibyl at Cuma. The guarantee for a safe return to Earth, could be assured by taking a branch of mistletoe as an offering to Persephone. Vergil tells how Aeneas was directed by the Sibyl to search in the forest for the Golden Bough (mistletoe) growing on a white poplar, and how he was helped in his search by turtle doves sent by his mother Aphrodite. Only if the suppliant was acceptable to Persephone could he pluck the branch from the tree, otherwise no knife or force could move it.

The Underworld formed the subject of innumerable paintings on vases and there was one very famous painting on the wall of the Temple of Apollo at Delphi, which unfortunately has disappeared. But Pausanias saw it during his tour of Greece in the first century A.D. Vergil also had probably seen it. Pausanias tells the story far better than I can, and here is his account.

The other part of the picture, the one on the left, shews Odysseus, who has descended into what is called Hades to enquire of the soul of Teiresias, about his safe return home. The objects depicted are as follows; there is water like a river clearly intended for Acheron with reeds growing in it; the forms of fishes appear so dim, that you will take them for shadows rather than fish. On the river is a boat with the ferryman at the oars. Polygnotus (the artist) followed I think the poem called Minyad. For in this poem occur lines referring to Theseus and Peirithoiis,

Then the boat on which embark the dead, that the old
ferryman Charon, used to steer, they found not at its moorings.

For this reason then Polygnotus too, painted Charon as a man well striken in years. Those on board the boat are not altogether distinguishable. Tellis appears as a youth in years, and Cleoboea as still a maiden, holding on her knees a chest such as they are wont to make for Demeter. All I heard about Tellis was that Archilochus the poet was his grandson, while as for Cleoboea, they say she was the first to bring the orgies of Demeter from Paros to Thasos.

On the bank of the Acheron under the boat of Charon, there is a notable group consisting of a man who had been undutiful to his father and is now being throttled by him. For the men of old held their parents in the greatest respect, as we may infer among other instances, from those in Catana called the pious, who when the fire flowed down from Aetna, held of no account gold or silver, but when they fled took up one his mother and the other his father. As they struggled on, the fire rushed up and caught them in the flames. Not even so would they put down their parents, and it is said the stream of lava divided itself in two and the fire passed on, doing no hurt to either young man or their parents. These Catanians even at the present time, receive honours from their fellow countrymen. Near the man in Polygnotus' picture who maltreated his father, and for this drinks his cup of woe in Hades, is a man who paid the penalty for sacrilege. The woman who is punishing him is skilled in poisons and in other drugs, so it appears that in those days men laid the greatest stress on piety to the gods. As the Athenians showed when they took the sanctuary of Olympian Zeus at Syracuse, they moved none of the offerings, but left the Syracusan priest as their keepers. Datis the Persian, too, showed his piety in his address to the Delians, and in this act as well, when having found an image of Apollo in a Phoenician ship he restored it to the Tanagraeans at Delos. So at that time all men held the divine in reverence, and that is why Polygnotus has depicted the punishment of him who committed sacrilege.

Higher up than the figures I have enumerated comes Eurynomus, said by the Delphian guides to be one of the Demons of Hell, who eats off all the flesh from the corpses leaving only the bones. But Homer's *Odyssey*, the poem called the *Minyad*, and the *Returns*, although they tell of Hades and its horrors, know of no demon called Eurynomus. However I will describe what he is like and his attitude in the picture. He is of a colour between blue and black, like that of meat flies. He is shewing his teeth and seated and underneath him is spread a vulture's skin. Higher up than the figures I have already quoted, are Perimedes and Eurylochus, companions of Odysseus, carrying victims for sacrifice, these are black rams. After them is a man seated, said by the inscription to be Oenus (Sloth). He is depicted as plaiting a cord and by him stands a she-ass eating up the cord as fast as he plaits it. They say this Oenus was a diligent man with an

extravagant wife. Everything he earned by working was quickly
spent by his wife. So they will have it, that Polygnotus has painted
a parable about the wife of Oenus. Oenus, too, is a name given
to a bird by the seers who observe birds that are ominous. This
Oenus is the largest and most beautiful of the herons, a rare bird
if ever there was one. Tityus too, is in the picture; he is no longer
being punished but has been reduced to nothing by continuous
torture, an indistinct and mutilated phantom.

And beyond Eriphyle have been painted Elpenor and
Odysseus. The latter is squatting on his feet, and holding his
sword over the trench, towards which the seer Teiresias is
advancing. After Teiresias, is Anticleia, the mother of Odysseus,
upon a rock. Elpenor has on, instead of clothes, a mat, such as
is usual for sailors to wear. Lower down than Odysseus are
Theseus and Peirithoüs sitting on chairs. The former is holding
in his hands the sword of Peirithoüs and his own. Peirithoüs is
looking at the swords and one might conjecture that he is angry
with them for having been useless and of no help in their daring
adventures. Panyassis the poet says, that Theseus and Peirithoüs
did not sit chained to their chairs, but that the rock grew to their
flesh and so served as chains. The proverbial friendship of
Theseus and Peirithoüs has been mentioned by Homer in both
his poems. . . .

Turning our gaze to the lower parts of the picture, we see next
after Patroclus, Orpheus, sitting on what seems to be a sort of
hill; he grasps with his left hand a harp, and with his right he
touches a willow. It is the branches that he touches and he is
leaning against the tree. The Grove seems to be that of Persephone, where grew as Homer thought, black poplars and willows.
The appearance of Orpheus is Greek and neither his garb nor his
headgear is Thracian. On the other side of the willow tree is
Promedon, leaning against it. There are some who think the name
Promedon was the poetic invention of Polygnotus, others have
said that Promedon was a Greek who was fond of listening to
all kinds of music, especially that of Orpheus. In this part of the
painting is Scedius who led the Phocians at Troy and after him
is Pelias, sitting in a chair with grey hair and a grey beard and
looking at Orpheus. Schedius is holding a dagger and is crowned
with grass. Tamyris is sitting with Pelias; he has lost the sight
of his eyes; his attitude is one of utter dejection; his hair and
beard are long; at his feet lies a broken lyre with its horns and
strings broken.[20]

The full description of the picture occupies no fewer than
thirteen pages of the Loeb translation of Pausanias. The picture seems to have been an epitome of Greek mythology, and

it shows what great importance was attached to the problem of life after death and the nature of the Underworld.

Although the story of Avernus covers these enormous periods of time, it all seems to culminate in the hundred years before the birth of Christ and perhaps another hundred years after. This is the epoch to which the discoveries that Keith Jones and I made at Baiae must be related. So before concluding this topographical picture of the region, I should give at least a sketch of Roman Baiae.

The first mention of Baiae with its healing waters, is by the historian Livy, who writes of the Consul Cneius Cornelius suffering from arthritis. He came to Baiae to take the *"aquae Cumanae"* and there built a villa, the remains of which are still, possibly, to be seen on the south side of the Bay. This was in 178 B.C. Before that Livy had also mentioned that in 209 B.C., when Hannibal was there, he had sacrificed at the Oracle of the Dead near Avernus. From this date onwards, the patricians and rich merchants of Rome seemed to vie with each other, as to who could build the most magnificent villa. Whilst nothing definite seems to be known of the origin of the Julian Family, they were amongst the first to come to Baiae and build their palace upon the cape forming the south point of the bay. It is quite likely that Julius Caesar was born here about 100 B.C.[21] Then began the glorious period for Baiae. Today as we visit the bay, we see terrace on terrace of vaulted houses covering the whole west wall of the crater that forms the bay. Detailed investigation of these ruins proves they are the remains of an old established town, much older than Roman Baiae. The architecture and town-planning are typical of the Etruscan and other Italiote hillside towns, examples of which can be seen on almost every isolated eminence in Southern Italy. The terraced town is, in fact, the old town which grew up round the ancient Sanctuary of Apollo and Oracle of the Dead which Keith and I found high up in the ruins.

The Romans came primarily for summer holidays and they built their houses down on the beach. The bay was dominated by the terrace town in the centre, the Palace of the Caesars on the south cape and on the north cape what in effect was their parish church, the Temple of Venus Lucrina. Owing to

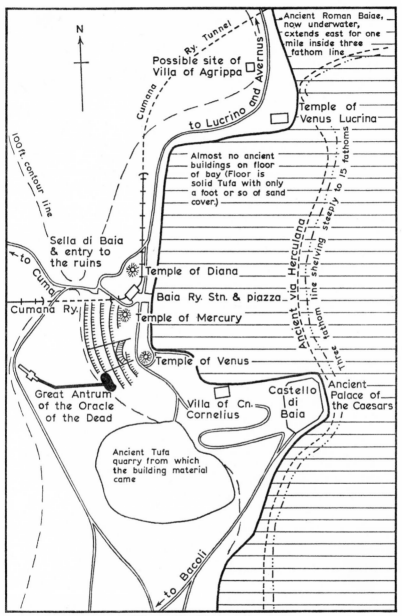

Fig. 2. THE BAY OF BAIA

the effects of bradyseism, the sea level was almost eighteen feet lower than it is today, and the shoreline followed closely the three-fathom line on today's chart. A glance at the map will show that there was dry land on the floor of the Bay of Baiae. The Via Herculana ran across from the Palace of the Caesars, direct to the Punta del'Epitaffio and the whole front of the bay was lined with a wonderful colonnade more than a mile long. These great Corinthian columns of white marble more than 45 feet high, carried a decorative pediment showing hunting, fishing, and country scenes. A number of fragments are preserved in the car park at the entrance to the 'Thermae'. On the landward side were gardens with swimming pools and fountains, sunbathing lawns and all the luxuries of Roman opulence.

From the end of the Punta del'Epitaffio, stretching towards Puteoli a couple of miles away, along the dyke separating Lake Lucrino from the sea, the beach was nearly half a mile wider than it is today. It was here that Roman society built the beach houses that ranged from the modest villa of Horace, the poet, to the villa of the mother of Nero.

Cicero was the local magnate; he owned many shops and other property in Puteoli, and doubtless was engaged in some of the merchant ventures based on the port. He was, as we all know, a very famous advocate and fortunately many of his speeches and literary works have survived. From his criminal cases we learn what sort of scandals arose amongst the high society at Baiae. Cicero was defending a young man, Marcus Celius, on a charge of attempted murder by poison of a woman he had met on the beach at Baiae. Cicero in the course of his speech for the defence, attacks the character of the woman and the vicious atmosphere of Baiae.

But, one may ask, is there not something strange about his approach to Clodia? Has public opinion nothing to say . . . nothing about the beaches at Baiae? Yes. They not only talk, but are well aware of the unbridled licentiousness of this woman, that has grown from furtive acts of loneliness performed in darkness, to performance in full daylight, in front of the whole world. . . . I will not mention names, but if a woman, who has no husband, opens her house to all who wish to enter, and openly carries on the life of a prostitute, by dining with strangers, and this at home

The author standing in the ruins of the Temple, at the entrance to the Great Antrum.

General view of the excavations of the hill-side town at Baiae looking south-west. The Temple and the Great Antrum are below the hill at left centre.

The Sacred Area at Baiae. From right to left are the reconstructed Painted Room, the Big "D", the Sudatorium, the Original Entrance and the Temple.

or in the town, and in the midst of the crowd at Baiae . . . and
if she comports herself not only in the way she walks, but in her
make up and in her companions . . . not only by flirtatious glances
and freedom of speech, but with kisses and embraces on the
beach, on board boats and at mealtimes, she thus clearly shows
herself to be a prostitute . . . and what is more, a bare faced
exponent of the trade.

His client was acquitted.[22]

Col. David Lewis, who has done some fine underwater research in the Bay of Naples, has interested himself in tracing
the shoreline of the coast between the Roman naval base at
Misenum and their new port, the Portus Julia, in Lakes Lucrinus and Avernus. The evidence is clear and conclusive. He
was able to trace the coastal road from the tunnel at the end of
Punta Pennata (Misenum) right along the three fathom line on
the chart. One of the incidental results was the fact that the
cliff line is the same today as ever. This was shown by the fact
that, although to all intents and purposes the road runs along
the foot of the cliff, it is only in one or two places, that there is
any quantity of detritus fallen from the cliff.

In the port of Misenum itself, there has been a fall of some
twenty feet from the cliff face into the water. Col. Lewis said
that he found a great quantity of small domestic items such as
lamps, pots and amphorae, marble tiles and mosaic, all debris
from the interior of rooms. "It would seem possible, that the
fall took place, probably as the result of a severe earthquake,
whilst the rooms were occupied. On the sea side of the road,
the bottom falls away steeply to the depths of 100 feet in many
places. The contour of the coast is seen to be a narrow shelf
running along the base of the cliffs at a depth today of some
15 to 20 feet, which level is maintained in the ruins of Roman
Baiae in the shallow water off the dyke separating Lake Lucrino from the sea. The strange thing about this is, that the level
of the water in Lake Avernus today is the same as it was in the
time of Agrippa, as the holes cut in the marble quay blocks for
mooring the ships, can still be seen at the appropriate level all
round the lake. It seems, therefore, that it was the floor of the
Gulf of Pozzuoli that sank, thus showing that it forms a crater
separate from the land.

In spite of the presence of the Roman emperors and the

D

majority of Roman high society every summer at Baiae for five hundred years, the number of references in Latin writers that tell us anything about the town are few indeed. Time has destroyed most of the great villas, and any reconstruction of the life of the times must be by inference. The presence of the Court at Baiae and the nearness of the great port of Puteoli, concentrated where the frontiers of Roman Italy, Magna Grecia and the Italiote tribes all met, make this area an ideal spot for archaeological research. Marble columns from Greece, Asia Minor and Africa formed the decoration for the villas. Wine amphorae from all the great centres of the wine trade in the Aegean, from the vineyards of Falernum and other places in Italy lie in thousands on the sea bottom, and in piles of broken sherds over the whole area. Strabo mentions hams from the south of France, fish from Spain, carpets and silks from the Orient, as some of the luxuries coming into Puteoli, for the entertainment of the holidaymakers at Baiae.

There is a fine satire on life in the Phlegrean Fields, written by Petronius, who was Nero's equerry responsible for the arrangement of his parties and other entertainments. It is believed to be the description or parody on a special feast given by the Emperor. The story is called *Satyricon* or the Feast of Trimalchio.

This Trimalchio is a freedman, that is to say an emancipated slave, who had, by devious practices, become so rich and owned so much land that he did not know the extent of his dominions. He has the ignorance of the uneducated, but insists on making pompous speeches all through the dinner, misquoting poets and mistaking his facts. The meal seems to have lasted all night, with a display of luxury that merits some description.

Here we are, then, at table. Boy slaves from Alexandria rinse our hands with ice water. Others kneel and wash our feet and pare our toenails with marvellous ingenuity. To crown all, whilst performing these ignoble tasks, they sing happily to themselves. After this they commenced to serve the hors d'oeuvre. These were served from a trolley, in the centre of which was a Corinthian bronze donkey with two panniers filled, one with green olives and the other with black. Over the donkey forming a kind of roof, were two heavy silver platters incised with the name of Trimalchio and their weight, decorated with garlands of sweetmeats made from poppies and honey. There was an imitation grill underneath, with small sausages upon it, the fire underneath being simulated by pomegranate seeds and black Syrian prunes. There were new-born mice preserved in honey, prawns, mussels and other shellfish and sea-foods, pickles, dried meats and hard-boiled eggs. Wines from Falernum and the finest vintages flowed freely. Then came an unexpected surprise, a great dish which drew the gaze of everyone for its novelty and mode of presentation. It was a triumph of the culinary art. A huge circular silver dish divided into the twelve signs of the Zodiac, held in each section, an appropriate confection. For Aries, a model in chick-pea meal of a horned goat. On the sign of the Bull, grilled sweet-breads, on Gemini grilled kidneys, on the Crab a crown, on Leo some African figs, on the Virgin a part of a sucking pig, on Libra a pair of scales, which carried in one pan a tart and in the other a 'pizza', on Scorpio was a small fish, on Sagittarius a crow, on Capricorn a crayfish, above the Aquarius a goose and on Pisces two red mullet. In the centre was a turf cut with its grass support-ing a honeycomb. An Egyptian boy slave carried the bread round to the guests in a silver basket. "Let us eat" cries Trimalchio. In ran slaves to raise the great circular dish and display beneath, whole roast fowls, boiled pork strips, and in its centre a hare with wings to represent Pegasus. At each corner were various containers of piquant sauces to pour over the dishes as they were served. The next course to appear was whole roast pig. The cook cut the stomach open and out poured yards and yards of sausages, and black puddings which caused much merriment amongst the guests.[23]

Certainly the Romans knew how to feed.

The Emperor Claudius built a beautiful new villa at Baiae for his wife Messalina. Caligula built a pontoon bridge of boats from the palace at Baiae to Puteoli, so that he could cross and visit his friends. In the little theatre at Baiae, in the centre of what we should call the balcony tier of seats, is a large alcove that I like to think was the royal box, quite handy to the ladies retiring room with dressing-table, wash basin and lavatory all complete. How often did Messalina or Cleopatra sit in that box and watch the performances on the stage beneath. Was it here that Messalina finally overstepped the limits of her excesses by being married on the stage to Silius and then and there con-summating the marriage in the public view? Wherever this occurred, it was the end so far as Claudius was concerned. He ordered her execution.

In Roman times Lucrino, Baiae, Bacoli and Misenum formed one continuous built up area. All the slopes and hills were covered with the luxurious villas of the patricians and there are many fascinating stories about the doings and goings on in these veritable palaces. Drusus built a villa for his wife Antonia at Bacoli, on the ridge overlooking the port of Misenum. Like all Romans, she was a firm believer in signs and portents. For the purpose of learning the future, she kept a school of Moray eels. These are fierce black eels about three feet long. They were bred in special hatcheries with mysterious rites connected with the constellation Draco. When the young eels were born, they were grouped in schools and placed in circular tanks. They were trained to swim round, always in the same direction. When the eels were consulted for an omen, the enquirer offered a titbit. If the eel took it all was well, but if the titbit was refused, the outlook was black indeed. Antonia provided her eels with golden earrings in their gills. The pool has survived and can still be seen in the villa on the Punta Pennata at Bacoli. Caligula afterwards poisoned Antonia for some reason. Later the villa became the property of Nero.

The following ghastly story, so dramatically told by Tacitus of the murder of his Mother Agrippina gives a lurid picture of Nero's brutality. He was made Emperor by the intrigues of his mother, who as the wife of the Emperor Claudius, induced him to declare Nero as his heir instead of his own son by Messalina. Agrippina was an overbearing woman who lived only for power. Eventually Nero became tired of her continual interference. So he decided she must be eliminated, but Agrippina was popular in Rome and Nero feared to carry out his crime there. Each year Nero went to Baiae for the Festival of Minerva, which was held on March 19th and lasted for five days. He invited Agrippina to meet him there telling his friends that "Parent's whims must be borne" and their feelings humoured, thus creating the impression that they were friends again. As she stepped ashore at Misenum from the ship that had brought her from Antium, Nero met her on the beach with outstretched arms and filial embraces. With effusive cordiality he conducted her to the villa on the hill, "to Bauli, a mansion on the bay between Cape Misenum and the waters of Baiae". Here she attended dinner with the Emperor. In the meanwhile a barge had been prepared with sumptuous fittings that was to take her to her villa at Lucrino. The roof of the cabin was loaded with lead weights and arranged to collapse and kill Agrippina. An informer warned her of the plot, so she requested to go to Lucrino by litter. But the party went on until the early morning with Agrippina in the place of honour next to Nero himself, who showered attentions upon her. She therefore forgot her alarm. When she finally left in the barge Nero embraced her again and "gazed long and affectionately into her eyes". Tacitus says, "This may have been his final piece of acting or perhaps even his brutal conscience was smitten at the sight of his mother going to her death."

On the barge Agrippina was attended only by two friends, Crepercius Gallus and a woman Acerronia. They happily discussed the re-establishment of good relations with her son. All of a sudden the roof of the cabin fell in and the heavy weights killed Crepercius instantly. Agrippina and Acerronia were saved by the sides of the couch which supported the weight of the roof. Seeing that the plot had failed, the oarsmen ran to one side and upset the barge. Acerronia called out, "I am Agrippina, save the Emperor's Mother". She was immediately struck down by many blows. Agrippina kept quiet and was unrecognised. Although her shoulder was injured, she swam to a sailing boat belonging to some fishermen, who took her to Lucrino. She realised that the invitation and the dinner had all been a plot to get her on the barge and encompass her death. It was a perfectly calm night and there were no rocks upon which the vessel could have been wrecked. Nevertheless she decided that the only way to escape the danger was to ignore it. She sent her freedman Agerinus to Nero to inform him "that by divine mercy and his lucky star she had survived a serious accident". He was also to say there was no need for Nero to visit her as she was resting to recover from her injury.

Nero was awaiting news of her death. Instead he heard of her escape from a situation, which could have left no possible doubt in her mind about the author of the attempt. He was terrified at the possibility that she would take revenge, "she may send her armed slaves or appeal to the army, or gain the ear of the Senate and accuse me of wrecking her vessel and killing her friends, what shall I do, What shall I do. . . ." He sent for

Seneca and Burrus to advise him. They remained silent for a long time. Then Seneca turned to Burrus and said to him that it might be advisable to send troops to execute her. Burrus replied that the Praetorian Guard were so loyal to the whole Royal House that they might refuse to carry out the order. Burrus said that the Prefect of the Fleet, Anicetus, had started the affair and he should finish it. Anicetus unhesitatingly accepted the task and Nero exclaimed, "This is the first day of my reign, and it is the gift of a former slave (Anicetus); go quickly, and take men who obey orders unscrupulously." At that moment Agrippina's messenger arrived, and Nero staged a faked incrimination. When Agerinus had delivered his message, Nero dropped a sword at his feet, and had him arrested as caught red-handed in an assassination attempt.

Meanwhile the people of Bacoli and Baiae had heard of Agrippina's escape and were preparing to stage a joyful demonstration at her villa. But the arrival of the armed execution party soon put a stop to this. Anicetus surrounded the villa and forced his way in. All the slaves were arrested and he reached her bedroom door. Here stood a few frightened servants and in the dimly lit room only a single maid waited on her. Her maid ran out of the room. "Are you leaving me, too," she cried and then she saw Anicetus and a naval captain and a lieutenant. "If you have come to visit me you can report that I am better, but if you are assassins, I know my son is not responsible, he would not order his mother's death."

Then the captain hit her on the head with a truncheon, and the lieutenant finished her off with his sword. Some say that Nero inspected the body afterwards, and had it cut open to see where he had come from. But this is contested. She was cremated lying on a couch without ceremony, and then given a modest tomb "beside the road to Misenum" on the heights where Julius Caesar's mansion overlooks the bay beneath. During the cremation one of her slaves stabbed himself to death, either for love of his mistress or because he feared assassination. This end had been anticipated for years by Agrippina, as she had been told by astrologers that her son would become Emperor, but he would kill her.

Nero only fully grasped the horror of his crime after it had been committed. For the whole of that night, he waited speechless and half paralysed with terror, not knowing what would happen. Hope returned when Anicetus returned and congratulated him on his happy escape from his mother's evil activities. Nero's friends crowded to the temples to offer sacrifices and demonstrations of joy to laud him. "Many prodigies occurred. A woman gave birth to a snake. Another woman was killed in her husband's arms by a thunderbolt. The sun suddenly went dark. All fourteen city districts were struck by lightning. But these portents meant nothing, so little were they due to the gods that Nero continued his reign and his crimes for years to come." That is how Tacitus records this black page of Bacoli's history.[24]

After the death of Nero, the villa remained the property of the Royal House. Vespasian also kept fish in Antonia's Pool, and it is said that each one came to him when called by name. Looking out over the port of Misenum is a little balcony or summerhouse of the villa, which has survived. I often go and sit there to conjure up the ghosts of the past.

Tiberius died here and so did Hadrian. Even from this chance information, it is clear that this region was the favourite dwelling place of Roman high society. The complication that is created by the fact that our reconstruction covers a period of three or four hundred years only serves to spotlight the importance this concentration of ruling families must have had on the future of the Roman Empire. Julius Caesar may have been born here. Certainly the Julian family were one of the first to become prominent in the Phlegrean Fields, and the first to build their great palace on the southern point of the Bay of Baiae. Caesar, undoubtedly, would have spent his summers here as did all Roman society.[25] Here, then, lived Cleopatra and their son Caesarion, from September 47 B.C. when they arrived from Egypt at Misenum, until the assassination of Caesar on the Ides of March 44 B.C. in the Senate House at Rome. It seems probable that Cleopatra was at Baiae at this time, as she was able to escape to Egypt. She had her ship either in the port of Misenum or at Puteoli. If she had been in Rome it seems unlikely that she would have lived or been allowed to get away.

Following the assassination of Julius Caesar the struggle for power broke out afresh, between Octavian and his supporters and the murderers of Caesar. Suetonius described these events in his *Lives of the Twelve Caesars*. Speaking of Octavian he says the "Sicilian war (against Pompey) lasted for eight years. It was interrupted by two storms that wrecked his fleets, and in summer too, and obliged him to rebuild them; also by the Pompeians success in cutting his corn supplies, which forced him to grant a popular demand for an armistice. At last, however, he got his new ships into fighting condition, with 30,000 freed slaves trained as oarsmen in the Julian Harbour formed at Baiae, by letting the sea into the Lucrine and Avernan Lakes. Here he exercised his crews all the winter and when the sailing season opened again, defeated Sextus Pompey off the Sicilian coast between Mylae and Naulochus, although on the eve of the battle he fell so fast asleep that his staff had to waken him and ask for the signal to begin hostilities. This must have been the occasion of Mark Antony's taunt, "He could not even stand up to review his fleet when the ships were already at their fighting stations, but lay on his back and gazed up at the sky, never rising to show if he was alive until Admiral Agrippa had routed the enemy." Augustus has been taken to task for crying out, "I will win this war whatever Neptune may do." This story sounds very much as if Octavian was a bad sailor and was prostrated with sea sickness during the battle.

When Octavian became Augustus Caesar, after the defeat of Mark Antony and the latter's suicide with Cleopatra, he spared the children of Antony and Cleopatra but had Caesarion killed, doubtless because he feared him as a possible rival.[26]

It was during this war that Admiral Agrippa suppressed the cult of Apollo and that of the gods of the Infernal Regions inside the crater of Avernus and at Baiae. The Roman Fleet was divided into two squadrons, one of which was based on Ravenna and the other at Misenum. Round the shores of the Lake of Misenum, many funeral steles have been found giving the names of Roman officers and even of the ships in which they served. The naval barracks were all along the shores of the lake and the sea dyke is still called Miliscola (The Recruit School), where the chief petty officers put the rookies through their squad drill.

The proximity of the port of Puteoli with its connections with the Near East would have provided many pilots with the knowledge of Greek and Egyptian waters which materially assisted in the winning of the battle of Actium in which Antony was defeated after being deserted by Cleopatra with her galleys. But Puteoli also seethed with unrest, due to the presence of hundreds of nationals from the conquered countries, most of whom believed in strange religions and all of whom were against the Roman authority. With the manpower shortage which had been overcome by emancipating slaves, Admiral Agrippa found that many of his new recruits were addicted to these strange religious beliefs, and insubordinate against authority. He dealt with this situation by suppression of all places where the religious rites were being performed. The punishment in the Roman forces for mutiny was decimation. Lots were drawn and every tenth man, innocent or guilty, was executed as an example to the others, to obey orders in future.

Agrippa cut down the sacred groves on the banks of the lake of Avernus and used the timber to build his ships. He built his dockyards on the sites of Apollo's shrines. Such sacrilege infuriated Apollo. His statue in the temple at Rome broke into sweat and he sent a great storm in the Bay of Naples that raged without ceasing until the Pontifex Maximus sacrificed a hecatomb of victims to appease him.[27] These happenings caused Agrippa to pause in his ruthless destruction and he was forced to take other measures to suppress the troubles. He did not destroy the Sanctuary of the Oracle of the Dead in the terraced town at Baiae, but he sealed off the underground sanctuary by blocking the access tunnels and he converted the surface buildings into a thermal establishment.

Keith and I found these blockages intact after two thousand years. We consider them of vital evidence for the identification of the Oracle. Unless the complex of tunnels was of great import, the Romans would never have undertaken so much work to camouflage the true uses of these galleries and chambers.

It was in this fascinating region that I came to live in 1960 and immediately fell under the spell of the mystery of the old ruins. I found that Baiae had been excavated in 1956-58 and the terraces of the ancient town brought to light again. Apart from this little research work had been done and there was practically no available information as to what Baiae might have looked like in its former glory. Here I met Keith Jones and we decided to try and reconstruct for ourselves, a picture of Roman life, when the villas at Bacoli and Baiae were the scenes of the banquets of Lucullus.

It is hard to credit the incredible cruelties described by Suetonius in his *Lives of the Twelve Caesars*. Nero murdered his mother for her oyster fisheries which he coveted. Countless others were executed as the result of false evidence, or on the most trivial accusations, especially if their crime was to be rich. To die a natural death in bed was a rare event; even for the Emperor himself assassination, enforced suicide, poisoning and torture; these were the background to the luxury and wickedness of Roman Baiae.

Every now and then we feel a slight earth tremor at Baiae to remind us of the unstable fires beneath. Looking out over the sea towards the east, Vesuvius dominates the far shore of the Bay of Naples. For ten years now the mountain has ceased to smoke. Recently however, it has begun to show signs that the next eruption is not far distant. Whenever I look at it I am reminded of Pliny's description of that awful day on 24th August, A.D. 79, when Pompeii was destroyed. Pliny the Elder was the Roman Admiral at Misenum. His nephew later wrote to his friend Tacitus the historian, telling of the eruption and how Admiral Pliny lost his life. He says:

It was 24th August, about seven o'clock in the morning, when my mother called our attention to a great black cloud, looking like an enormous pine tree. My uncle ordered a trireme to be got ready and he went to try to rescue the people living along the coast at the foot of the mountain. The closer they approached to the shore, the thicker became the clouds of hot ashes and cinders falling on the deck. The Steersman wished to retreat, but Pliny decided to push on to Stabiae, to the villa of his friend Pomponiasus.

Meanwhile the mountain seemed to be a mass of flames and fires at all points, the flashes of the flames only intensified the blackness of the night.

Pliny went to sleep in a room in the villa, but soon the slaves awakened him because the fall of ashes was blocking the doorways. They all went down to the beach to try and escape to the ship. But the wind had changed and there was too heavy a sea breaking on the beach. They waited throughout the night in clouds of poisonous sulphurous gas. Pliny who suffered from asthma, could not resist any more, he fell down and died.

Meanwhile at Misenum young Pliny and his mother were having a terrible time also. The earthquakes were terrific; all the houses were destroyed and the ground was heaving up and down. Carts were rolling back and forth on level ground, such was the violence of the movements. The air was full of grey powdered ash; they could not see where they were going, but they joined the crowd and tried to escape. The fury of the eruption endured for twenty-four hours. When at last they were able to see through the clouds of ash and first light of dawn of the second day, the whole countryside was covered nearly a foot deep in ash looking like snow.[28]

The amount of material blown away in the eruption was enormous. The roof of the Sanctuary of Hera at the mouth of the River Sele, over eighty miles to the south of Vesuvius collapsed under the weight of ash deposited upon it. I calculated that before the eruption the original mountain must have been a cone over nine thousand feet high to provide such a quantity of dust. Death was instantaneous when a blast of hot gas struck. Amongst the pathetic relics at Pompeii, is the cast of the body of the Roman sentry at the gate of the city. The blast caught him as he bent down to cover his dog with his cloak in an effort to protect him.

Incidents like these can be found everywhere in the Campania, but Keith and I felt there was a deeper significance in the concentration of population round Baiae, especially in the period from 190 B.C. to A.D. 100.

NOTES

1. *Horace*, Epist. 1, 83.
2. *Martial*, Elegy, *passim*.
3. A. W. Gunther, *Illustrated London News*, January 1964.

4. Suetonius, *The Twelve Caesars*, Domitian.
5. Pliny the Elder, *Historia Naturalis*, Description of the Italian coast.
6. Livy, XLI, 16.
7. Strabo, V, 4-5.
8. Homer, *Odyssey*, XI. Opening lines.
9. Homer, *loc. cit.*
10. A. Maiuri, *The Phlegrean Fields* (Italian Government) page 114.
11. P. G. Sestieri, *Guide to Paestum* (Italian Government).
12. Pausanias, XXVIII, *passim.*
13. Herodotus, VII, 169.
14. Vergil, *Aeneid*, III. 600 *seq.*
15. Homer, *Odyssey*, last 70 lines Bk. X and opening lines XI.
16. Strabo, V, 4, 8.
17. Strabo, *loc. cit.*
18. A. Maiuri, *op. cit.*, page 108 *seq.*
19. Hesiod, *Theogony*, *passim.*
20. Pausanias, XXVIII-XXXI.
21. Suetonius, *The Twelve Caesars*, Julius Caesar.
22. Cicero, *Pro Celio.*
23. Petronius, *Satyricon*, *passim.*
24. Tacitus, *Annals of Imperial Rome*, Nero.
25. A. Maiuri, *op. cit.*, page 156.
26. Suetonius, *The Twelve Caesars*, Augustus.
27. Servius, *On Vergil's Georgics.*
28. Pliny the Younger, *Letters to his friends*, VI, 16 and 20.

2

Orpheus and His Deeds

The Greek religion was composed of two great sections, the original worship of the Chthonic gods of the Pelasgians, and the Olympic Gods. The Pelasgians were the first inhabitants of the region and 'Chthonic' is a Greek word meaning 'of the soil'. All the female deities were of the old religion and a great many of the rites were reminiscent of the ancient matrilineal societies. There is no need for me to enlarge on the roles of Zeus and Apollo, Athene, Aphrodite and the rest. Their story has been told so often that it must be known to everybody. What may not be quite so well-known are the rites of some of the ancient deities. There are two reasons for this. First because it seems that with the coming of the Olympians the old religions were proscribed. The result was that their rites were carried out in secret and survived as 'The Mysteries'. These were great initiation ceremonies in honour of the ancient gods. The principal Mysteries were those in honour of Demeter at Eleusis, those held at Thebes in honour of the Kabeiri and finally those of Dionysius. The ceremonies were secret and such was the veneration in which they were held, that no Greek writer ever violated the secrecy.

Even Vergil, a Roman, when he came to write the *Aeneid* and to speak of the secrets of the Underworld, asks pardon of the Gods. "Gods whose dominion over Souls, Shades without sound, Void and you Burning River, and you Broad Spaces voiceless beneath the Night, may I remain sinless in telling what has been told to me, and by your divine assent, reveal truth sunk in the depths of gloom."

The daily life of the Greek was ruled absolutely by the need

61

for religious observances to propitiate the gods for some error
or omission, or to ensure success in future undertakings. Signs,
portents and omens were interpreted by the diviner and believed
by everyone, absolutely. Life was lived for the joys it gave on
this Earth, there was little thought for what might be beyond
the grave. The Elysian Fields were reserved for heroes and sons
of the gods. The ordinary man died and his shade descended to
the Underworld, there to remain a witless, disembodied spirit
fluttering to and fro.

It was here that a new concept arose in religious thought
amongst the Greeks, which the philosophers ascribed to
Orpheus.

The fame of this great man will live for ever. Nevertheless he
has not yet received his full due. He is said to have brought
the Mysteries to Europe from Egypt and to have instituted the
dawn of belief in eternal life. He it was, who first realised the
spirituality behind the Egyptian theology and clothed it with
a symbolism that the ordinary man of his day could understand.
Christianity probably owes more to Orpheus than to many a
minor prophet of the Old Testament; in fact he deserves to rank
amongst the greatest of the prophets. His concepts were so close
to those of Christianity, that all the thunder of the first century
Christian Fathers was directed against his speech, and the suppression of his claims to fame.

The greatest authority on Orpheus is W. K. C. Guthrie and
the reader is directed to his book *Orpheus and the Greek Religion*, for a full exposition of this fascinating subject.

From the time of Homer onwards, there are constant references to Orpheus, yet when real information about the man
himself is sought, he turns out to be most elusive. The Greeks
believed him to be a real man; some dated him in the age of
heroes several generations before the time of Homer. But Herodotus is very definite when he says, "I am of opinion that
Homer and Hesiod lived four hundred years before my time and
not more. These are they who framed a theogony for the Greeks
and gave names to the gods and assigned to them honours and
arts and declared their several forms. But the poets said to have
been before them, in my opinion were after them." One of the
most reliable Greek writers was Pausanias and he undoubtedly believed that Orpheus had lived but he was sceptical

about some of the legends attached to his name. He says,

There are many untruths believed by the Greeks, one of which is that Orpheus was the son of the Muse Calliope and not of the daughter of Pireus (there are some who say that Pireus had nine daughters, and that their names were the same as the goddesses and that those are they that the Greeks call the children of the Muses, but they were the sons of the daughters of Pireus), that the beasts of the field followed him fascinated by his songs, and that he went down alive into Hades to ask for his wife from the Gods below. In my opinion Orpheus excelled his predecessors in the beauty of his verse, and reached a high degree of power because he was believed to have discovered mysteries for the purification of sins, cure of diseases and the means of diverting divine wrath.

But they say that the women of the Thracians plotted his death, because he persuaded their husbands to accompany him on his wanderings, but dared not carry out their intention, through fear of their husbands. Flushed with wine however they dared the deed, and thereafter the custom has been for their men to march into battle drunk. Some say that Orpheus came to his end by being struck by a thunderbolt, hurled at him by Zeus, because he revealed sayings in the Mysteries to men who had not heard them before. Others have said that his wife died before him, and that for her sake he came to Aornon in Thesprotis, where of old there was an Oracle of the Dead. He thought, they say, that the soul of Eurydice followed him, but turning round he lost her and committed suicide for grief. The Thracians say that such nightingales as nest on the tomb of Orpheus, sing more loudly and sweeter than the others.[1]

Diodorus Siculus, a historian who lived in the first century A.D. says,

Orpheus brought from Egypt, most of his mysteries, ceremonies and orgies, that always accompanied his wanderings. His fabulous story of his visit to Hades also came from Egypt. The rites of Osiris are the same as those of Dionysius and those of Demeter, the same as those of Isis with only the names changed. The punishment in Hades, of the Unrighteous and the Fields of Joy for the Righteous, all were introduced by Orpheus in imitation of Egyptian Funeral customs, together with all other conceptions current amongst the Greeks. Hermes, for instance, the Conductor of Shades according to the ancient Egyptian custom, brings the body of Apis the Bull to a certain place and there hands it over to one who wears the mask of the Hell-hound (Cerberus).[2]

Apollonius of Rhodes wrote the story of the voyage of the good ship *Argo*, in which Jason and his friends set out to bring back the Golden Fleece. In giving the list of distinguished heroes who made up the crew, he says,

> The name which I put first is that of Orpheus, born so the story goes, by Calliope to her Thracian lover Oeagrus, near the heights of Pimplea. They say that with the music of his voice, he enchanted stubborn mountain rocks and rushing streams. And testifying still to the magic of his song, there are wild oaks growing at Zone on the coast of Thrace, which he lured down from Piera with his Lyre, rank upon rank of them like soldiers on the march. Such was Orpheus, Lord of Distonian Pieria, when Jason, son of Aeson, acting on a word from Cheiron, enrolled him as a partner in his venture.

When they were about to depart on the voyage, they feasted far into the night and one named Ida got drunk and became quarrelsome.

> He spoke in anger with the will to wound, and the quarrel would have gone still further, had not their comrades, checked the contending pair with loud remonstrances. Jason himself intervened. And so did Orpheus, raising his lyre in his left hand, he leapt to his feet and began a song.
>
> He sang of the past age, when Earth and Sea and Sky were knit together in a single mould, how they were sundered after deadly strife, how the Stars, the Moon, and the travelling Sun keep faithfully to their stations in the Heavens, how mountains rose and how, together with their nymphs, the murmuring streams and all four-legged creatures came to be. How in the beginning Ophion and Eurynome, the daughter of Ocean, governed the world from snow-clad Olympus, how they were forcibly supplanted, Ophion by Cronos, Eurynome by Rhea; of their fall into the waters of Ocean, and how their successors ruled the happy Titan gods, when Zeus in his Dictaean Cave was still a child, with childish thoughts, before the Earth-born Cyclops had fortified him with the Bolt, the Thunder and Lightning that form his glorious armament today.
>
> The song was finished and his celestial voice had ceased together. Yet, even so there was no change in the company, the heads of all were still bent forward, their ears intent on the enchanting melody. Such was his charm—the music lingered in their hearts. But presently they mixed the libations that pious ritual prescribes for Zeus, poured them out on the burning

(*Right*) Entrance to a Cimmerian argilla ; (*below*) Paget inside the Cimmerian argilla. These caves were the "cells" and other living quarters of the priests who served the Oracle. They never saw the light of day, being permitted to go out only after sunset and before dawn.

The Temple as it exists today. Note the great rectangular blocks with which it was constructed.

(*Left*) The Grotto in the Temple over the entrance to the Great Antrum.

tongues (the smouldering embers of the sacrificial fire), and then in the dark betook themselves to sleep.[3]

On another occasion Orpheus saved the ship from foundering in a gale, by calming the fury of the storm-gods with his song.

Apollonius also says of Orpheus.

After he had devoted his entire youth to education, and learned whatever the myths had to say about the Gods, he went to Egypt where he further increased his knowledge and became the greatest man amongst the Greeks, both for his knowledge of the gods, as well as for his poems and songs. And because of the love for his wife, he dared the amazing deed of descending into Hades, where he enchanted Persephone with his melodious song and persuaded her to assist him in his desire to allow him to bring back his dead wife from Hades to Earth.

When assessing the meaning of the myths, it is always necessary to note the etymology of the words forming the names of places and of the persons concerned. In the case of the Orpheus story the termination *eus* indicates that his name is pre-Hellenic, possibly Mycenean or Cretan, then again, the name of his wife Eurydice is one of the titles of the Great Universal Goddess in pre-Olympic times. The word means 'universal justice' and immediately suggests connection with the religious concepts that Orpheus promulgated.

I have referred to the elusive nature of the information on Orpheus, the man, but there is a wealth of material to draw upon dealing with his religious ideas.

The great period of literary and philosophical activity, beginning about the sixth century B.C. and known to history as 'Classical Greece' was the time when much study was being given to both scientific and metaphysical problems. The poems of Homer were collected and codified into the form in which we know them. The teachings of Orpheus also came under review and were restated by Onomacritus at Athens, and by Pythagoras in Italy. Some say that these two men were really the authors of the concepts, but there seems to be too much contrary evidence that Orpheus had been known long before this, to make this view acceptable.[4]

E

It seems certain that Orphism was not a new religion, but a new concept of man, his origin and his destiny. A brief description of Orpheus' conception of the Universe and of Creation and Eternity will help show what a profound thinker he must have been.

The concepts of Orpheus were contained in writings that are now all but lost to us; only fragments remain. These were the Orphic hymns and the Orphic rhapsodies. In the Orphic *Rhapsodia*, there was the One Unutterable Principle out of which was born a mud that was to become Earth and Water. From these were born Cronos (Time), the great God that rules over the whole Universe. From Cronos were born Aether, and Erebus a yawning black bottomless abyss. In the Aether, Cronos fashioned a Silver Egg, which split in two and Phanes was born. Phanes has many names, such as Eros, Protogonos, Erikepaios, Netis and Dionysius. There is not enough left of the *Rhapsodia* to give the full story of Phanes and the Creation. We are told, there were men in those days, not like our men but giants, men of the Golden Age when the gods lived on earth.[5]

Night was the daughter of Phanes and also his wife. She bore him Uranus (Heaven) and Gea (Earth). From this point the Creation and theogony of Orpheus and that of Homer and Hesiod are identical, except for one very important deviation.

In the Orphic Principles there was One God, and only One God and it was therefore necessary that Phanes should also have created Man. How he did this is lost to us, but in order to bring things into line when the Olympians came, the myth says that Zeus swallowed the Creation of Phanes and then did it all over again. In the new order, the creation of man was made part of the myth of Dionysius, who was adopted as the God of the Orphics.

We always think of Dionysius as the wine god, whose rites were wild processions of intoxicated men and women (Maenads), culminating in sordid scenes of sexual licence. But we forget that our views on morality in the twentieth century are not the same as those of ancient Greece. In spite of the crudity of the Dionysian rites, they were the first conception of the idea of communion with their god. The sacrificial animal represented the God and by tearing it to pieces and eating the raw flesh the celebrants actually became part of the God. The Orphics adopted Dionysius as their God, because of the attributes he possessed.

Diodorus Siculus informs us, "This God (Dionysius) they say, was the son of Zeus and Persephone, and was born in Crete. Orpheus in his religious writings represents him, as being torn in pieces by the Titans." Pausanias also refers to the matter and says, "The Titans were first introduced into poetry by Homer, who said they were gods occupying a place under what is called Tartarus. Onomacritus took over the name of the Titans from Homer and founded the rites in honour of Dionysius, making the Titans to be for Dionysius, the authors of his sufferings."

The myth says, that Hera being jealous of the infidelity of Zeus plotted with the Titans to murder the child Dionysius. They distracted his attention by giving him various toys, such as spinning tops, a flock of raw wool, some jointed dolls, a ball, knuckle bones, apples and a mirror. Having killed him, they cut the body into strips and boiled them in milk, then proceeded to eat them in a cannibal feast. Athene who had taken part in the plot with the intention of betraying it to Zeus, saved the heart of Dionysius. She brought it to Zeus who placed it in his thigh and in due course Dionysius was born again. Zeus divided the dominions of the world between Dionysius and Apollo. Apollo was given the more serious role of law and order, medicine and justice, while Dionysius was concerned with agriculture and civilisation generally. After he had travelled all over the world carrying out his mission, he ascended to Olympus where he sits at the right hand of Zeus, in the seat which was given him by Hestia, the goddess of hearth and home.[6]

Guthrie says the central point of the Orphic story for a worshipper was the "Tales of Dionysius and his sufferings". He goes on to point out that it was the Cretan Dionysius, Son of Cretan Zeus, who was murdered.

The Cretans made the day of his death into a religious festival and founded a yearly rite, with triennial dedication, performing in order all that the child in his death both did and suffered. They tore a live Bull to pieces with their teeth, recalling the cruel feast in their annual celebration, and by discordant cries through

the depths of the forest, they imitated the ravings of an un-
balanced mind, in order that it might be believed, that the awful
crime was committed not by guile but in madness. Before them
was borne the chest in which the sister secretly stole away the
heart and with the sound of flutes and the clashing of cymbals
they imitated the rattles by which the boy was deceived.

The rise of the phenomenon known as Orphism, presents an
entirely different problem from that of any individual myth or
rite, whether it be the one used by the Orphics or not. All the
evidence points to its having been in its origin the product of a
few individual minds active over a limited period of time. We
need not therefore hesitate to speak in this way of Orpheus and
the Orphics, and may conclude that they meditated on the religious elements which I have described as existing before their
time, and either invented to suit their own purposes, a story of
the infant Bacchus (Dionysius), surrounded by a crowd of leap-
ing demons, or at least remodelled an existing one. It was they
who said the child was attacked by the Titans, and that his guard
proved insufficient and that the Titans killed him and ate his
flesh. If there were already in existence an aetiological tale of the
slaying of the god, the eating of the flesh no doubt formed part
of it, since it was an action of the Bacchants. The essential thing
is that the Orphics added the Titans. When Zeus made war on
the Titans, as everyone knew from Hesiod, his weapons were his
thunderbolts and lightnings. With these he burned up the earth
around them and the hot smoke scorched and defeated them.
To have as many familiar elements as possible in their story was,
very naturally, the aim of the Orphics, and here was one, that
suited their purpose admirably. Zeus attacks the Titans fresh
from their crimes, with his well known weapons. They are burned
up and from their ashes spring the race of men. The climax is
original, is Orphic (and in all this our evidence concurs) because
it enshrines the peculiarly Orphic thought of our mixed earthly
and heavenly nature.

The Orphics considered that man had been created from the
ashes of the Titans and that Phanes had breathed into each
one, his individual 'soul'. By conforming with the precepts of
Orpheus and leading a life of asceticism the soul would eventually be granted eternal life in the Elysian Fields.

The Underworld was an essential stage in the saga. When a
person died his Shade was immediately conducted to the Underworld by Hermes, the Conductor of Shades. Here his life on
earth was judged by three judges appointed by Zeus. Their
names were Rhadamanthus, Aecus and Minos.[7] Their investi-

gation was not concerned with his life in the moral sense as we know it today. It was strictly confined to ascertaining that all religious observances had been promptly carried out by the deceased. No one was perfect as their very origin was half earthly. They had had opportunity during their earthly life to acquire virtue in some measure and at the same time, maybe, certain evils had attached themselves to the soul. This evil could be purged by punishment and association with the god, assisted by communion, until the soul could pass into the Elysian Fields, there to await reincarnation and another journey on Earth, which eventually, after they had sojourned thrice in the Elysian Fields, to reunion with Phanes.

Greek writers are faithful to their oaths of secrecy, which they took at initiation into the Mysteries and it is extremely difficult to know what happened at these ceremonies.[8] Diodorus Siculus says, "In agreement with this, it is pointed out, are the expositions in the Orphic Poems and the things that are introduced into the Mysteries, the details of which it is not lawful to recount to the uninitiated". Pausanias says, "Whoever has been to an initiation at Eleusis, or read the writings called Orphic knows what I mean."[9] From this and other evidence, Guthrie thinks, that reading from the Orphic literature must have formed a major part of the initiation into the Orphic Mysteries. Euripides in his play *The Cretans*, makes the chorus say,

Son of the Phoenician Princess, Child of Tyrean Europa and Great Zeus, Ruler over hundred fortressed Crete—here am I, come from the sanctity of temples roofed with cut beam of our native wood, its true joints of Cypress welded together with Chalybean axe and cement from the Bull. Pure has my life been since I became an initiate of Idaean Zeus and herdsman of night-wandering Zagraeus, and having accomplished the raw feasts and held torches aloft to the Mountain Mother, yes torches of the Curetes, raised to the Holy Estate and called Bakhos.

"Clothed in raiment all white, I shun the birth of men, nor touch the coffins of the dead, and keep myself from eating food that had had life." So runs another fragment of *The Cretans*, which has given us so much information on Orphism. The Orphic held that this life was a punishment for some sin committed in the past.[10] The dogmas were a doctrine of personal salvation, when by a life of asceticism the contamination of the soul would gradually be removed and the person become a god again (as he was before the soul sinned). It was in this respect that the Orphic dogma differed from the Christian. There was also no provision to help one's neighbour to salvation, no community spirit as in the Christian congregation. The Christian believes solely in the Christian dogmas. The Orphic could be an initiate of several other religions if he so desired. Indeed it seems that there was a tendency in Classical times, to believe that initiation into one of the major Mysteries would guarantee a life with the Blest after Death. Many a man would feel that a double insurance by more than one initiation was worth taking out.

Dogma and precept were laid down in the Hymns and the Rhapsodia. There was a god who created all things, and the story of the origin of man, which had the doctrine of impurity and original sin. The precepts were directed towards a perfect union with the god by the elimination of original sin. The presence of the god is always within us, but is masked by impurity. The precepts include an ascetic way of life and doubtless regular attendance at sacrificial communions with the god-ancestor and Saviour Dionysius. At these meetings choral singing of Hymns and reading from the literature to remind the faithful of their duties, must have been the rule. As the Orphics would not take life, the rending of the sacrifice would have been done by mime, probably by the breaking of barley cakes and the ritual drinking of wine.

Initiation was the all important thing. The initiate was known as *Bakchos*, and when after death, he arrived at the Gates of Hades, he was, of course, in a privileged position. From time to time certain thin gold plates have been found in tombs in Southern Italy and in Crete, with verses on them. These verses were obviously taken from a longer context and their purpose is clear. They are a kind of passport to the Underworld with instructions as to how to proceed. Most of them were lying beside the corpses, but one from Petalia in Southern Italy, was rolled up in a little gold cylinder and hung round the neck of the corpse on a chain. This plate reads:

Thou shalt find to the left of the House of Hades, a Spring,

And by the side thereof stands a white cypress;
To this Spring approach not near.
But thou shalt find another from the Lake of Memory
Cold water flowing forth, and there are guardians before it.
Say "I am a Child of Earth and Starry Heaven;
But my race is of Heaven (Alone). This ye know yourselves.
But I am parched with thirst and I perish, Give me quickly
The cold water flowing from the Lake of Memory."
And of themselves they will give thee to drink of the Holy Spring
And thereafter, among the other Heroes thou shalt have lordship.

Another plate from Crete reads:

I am parched with thirst and I perish—nay drink of me
The ever flowing Spring on the right where the Cypress is.
Who art thou?
Whence art thou?—"I am the Son of Earth and Starry Heaven."

Later when we come to describe in detail the tunnels and galleries of the Oracle of the Dead, we shall see how the features correspond with the directions given in the plates. A plate from Thurii, Southern Italy, now in the Museum at Naples, has the following verses on it:

But as soon as the spirit has left the light of the Sun
Go to the right as far as one should go, being right wary in all
    things,
Hail, Thou who hast suffered the sufferings. Thou hadst never
    suffered before.
Thou art become god from man.
A kid thou art fallen into milk.
Hail, Hail to thee, journeying the right road
By Holy Meadows and Groves of Persephone.

There are three more plates in the Museum at Naples all bearing much the same formula. Guthrie quotes the following reconstruction by Professor Murray:

I come from the Pure, Pure Queen of those below
And Eukles and Eubuleus, and other gods and Daemons;
For I also avow that I am of your bledded race.
And I have paid the penalty for deeds unrighteous,
Whether it be that Fate laid me low or the Gods Immortal,
Or, with far-flung Thunderbolt
I have flown out of the sorrowful weary circle. I have passed
With swift feet to the Diadem desired.

I have sunk beneath the bosom of the Mistress, The Queen of
  The Underworld.
And now I come as a suppliant to Holy Persephone,
That of her grace she send me up to the seats of the Hallowed.
Happy and Blessed One, Thou shalt be god instead of Mortal.
A kid thou art fallen into milk.[11]

That these are Orphic, there cannot be the slightest doubt.
"I am a Child of Earth and Starry Heaven, but my race is of
Heaven" is the claim made by the Orphic to be the descendant
of the Titans, who were the sons of Uranus (Heaven) and Ge
(The Earth). The distinction between the two fountains, that on
the left being unlucky, is most interesting. There are two D-
shaped baths at Baiae in the Sacred Area, that may well symbol-
ise these two fountains of Forgetfulness and Memory. Also the
injunction to take the right road and so reach "The holy
meadows and Groves of Persephone", finds its counterpart at
the "Dividing of the Ways", in the great Antrum of the Oracle
of the Dead that Keith and I found at Baiae. I shall refer to this
again in my description of the Oracle in Chapter IV. The curious
expression, 'a kid I have fallen into milk', may refer to the boiling of the dismembered body of Dionysius in the cauldron of
milk by the Titans, or it may be just a repetition of a Greek pro-
verb having the same significance as the English one 'being born
with a silver spoon in one's mouth'. The line, "I have sunk
beneath the bosom of the Mistress, the Queen of the Underworld", refers to the suppliant's initiation. Being embraced by
the Goddess, or by a woman, holding the child (or initiate) so
that his head rested just below her breasts was the rite of
adoption into the family. "I have flown out of the sorrowful
weary circle" is a reference to some part of the initiation ceremony. According to that great authority on Greek religion,
Jane Harrison, pictures of the Underworld on a series of vases
in the Naples Museum all show a wheel hanging up, but what
the actual ceremony was is not known.

We owe most of our information about Orpheus, to the early
Christian Fathers, especially Clement of Alexandria. They
were so concerned to prove the pagan beliefs wrong, that they
went into a wealth of detail which otherwise would have been
lost to us. In this way we know that Orphism was a very
popular cult in Roman times and this, of course, means that it

must have been prevalent among the intelligentsia at Baiae. Supporting this, there was found some years ago, a funeral plaque at Cuma, bearing the words "None but Bakchoi may be buried here". What we may conclude from this is that there may have been a special part of the necropolis set aside for Orphics. If this is so they must have existed in considerable numbers in the region.

Cicero lived at Puteoli, and naturally was aware of what went on around him. In his work *On the Nature of the Gods*, he makes reference to Dionysius and the prevalence of Orphism. Vergil cannot have been alone in his adherence to the cult. All the evidence, sparse though it is, points to intense intellectual activity amongst the dwellers in the Phlegrean Fields in that period 100 B.C. to A.D. 100 and many must have been Orphics.

Plato pointed out in *Phaedra*, that "many carry the wand but few become Bakchoi", implying that the wild licence of the Dionysius processions attracted many others than true believers. But this is the same in every religion with spectacular rites.

There do seem to have been certain degrees in the cult itself. For instance Guthrie calls attention to certain inscriptions from Pergamon. These mention *Bakchoi* as the Initiated, *Mystai* and *Daduchoi* as the hierophants, *Bukuloi* as priests, and *Archibukulos* as the Supreme Pontiff of the cult. The word *Bukulos* means 'Ox-herd', but in spite of its strangeness, it has a parallel with the modern pastor, or shepherd. Then it must be remembered that their God, Dionysius was worshipped in the form of a bull.

It does appear as though the gold plates were something special. These plates were evidently given to men who had led lives of exceptional Orphic purity, and who were therefore considered to have "paid the penalty for deeds unrighteous" and to be ready for the supreme reunion with the godhead and become a god himself—an Orphic saint, in fact. It would also appear that there were two categories of inhabitants of the Elysian Fields, those awaiting a further reincarnation to earthly life and those about to ascend to the stars.

The gold plates form a fitting introduction to Anchises' speech in Book VI of the *Aeneid*, where Vergil not only demonstrates that he, himself, was an Orphic, but gives a graphic summary of the Orphic beliefs in the Underworld.

In order to ensure that the Sibyl and Aeneas could return safely back to Earth from their visit to Hades, Aeneas had provided himself, as instructed by the Sibyl, with a branch of mistletoe (the Golden Bough) as an offering to Persephone. So let us take up the story with their arrival at the door of the House of Persephone.

They kept pace together along the dimly lighted way, quickly crossed the space between and came near to the door. Swiftly Aeneas gained the entrance, sprinkled himself with holy water and set the branch upright on the threshold before him.

When this was done, their duty to the Goddess was fully discharged. And now they arrived at the Land of Joy, the pleasant green places in the Fortunate Woods, where are the Homes of the Blest. Here, an ampler air clothes the plains with brilliant light, and always they see a sun and stars which are theirs alone. Of these bright spirits, some were taking exercise together on the Field of Play, or wrestling on the yellow sand. Others were treading a rhythmic dance and as they danced they sang. And there too was Orpheus the Thracian Seer attired in his trailing gown, who answered their rhythm on seven intervals of notes, striking out the melody, now with fingers and now over again, with an ivory plectrum. Here was Teucer's ancient dynasty, that family of noble beauty, high hearted heroes born in happier years, Ilus, Assaracus and Dardanus, the founder of Troy. Aeneas looked in wonder at their arms and chariots resting idle there before him. Their spears stood planted in the ground; their horses were grazing free about the plain. For the same pleasure in chariots and arms which they knew in life and the same old interest in tending glossy horses, remain with them still, after they have been laid to repose in earth.

And Lo, Aeneas saw others to his right hand and to his left about the grass, feasting and singing a joyful hymn of praise in their choir. They were in the midst of a wood of scented bay trees, when the full-flowing River Eridanus goes rolling through forest land to the upper world. Here dwells a band who sustained wounds whilst fighting for their homelands, others who, whilst life was theirs, were priests without sin, or faithful seers whose speech never brought Apollo shame; some who had given life an added graciousness by inventions of skill and some who had made others remember them by being kind. All of them wore snow white ribbons circling their brows. And they all thronged round and the Sibyl spoke to them, especially to Musaeus who was the centre of a very large gathering, towering by head and shoulders above the rest, and all looked up to him. "Tell us Souls in Bliss, and especially you most gentle poet, in which district is Anchises and in which part of it may he be found? For it is to find him, that we have come, crossing the great rivers of Erebus." The hero answered her quickly in a few words, "No one has a fixed home. We live in shady woods and lie here on soft river banks, or dwell in meadows that the streamlets ever keep fresh. But if the wish in your hearts so inclines, climb this slope and I shall set you on an easy pathway." As he spoke he stepped ahead and from the higher ground on which they stood, showed them the glittering lands below. So they descended from the heights.

Now Anchises, his father, was passing under a thoughtful devoted survey of certain souls, who were then penned deep in a green vale, but destined to ascend to the upper light. For it chanced that he was reviewing the whole company of his line, his own grandsons to be and the destiny and fortune that would be theirs, their character and their deeds. But seeing Aeneas hastening over the grounds towards him, he stretched out both hands to him in his delight. Tears started down his cheeks and a cry broke from him. "You have come at last. . . . Your Father knew you would be true. So your faithfulness has overcome the hard journey. May I really look at your face, Son and hear the tones I know so well and talk with you. I did in fact expect from my reckoning that so it would be, for I computed the required passage of time. And my calculations did not deceive me. But to think of all the vast seas and lands that you have had to traverse, and all the perils of your storm-tossed journey, before I could welcome you at last! How I feared too that the Royal Power of Africa might do some hurt to you."

Aeneas answered, "Father, it was ever the vision of yourself, so often mournfully appearing to me, which compelled me to make my way to the threshold of this world. My fleet lies moored on the Etruscan brine. Father, Oh let me clasp your hand . . . do not slip from my embraces." As he spoke his face grew wet with the streams of tears. Three times he tried to clasp his arms about his Father's neck, but three times the clasp was in vain and the wraith escaped his hands, like airy winds or the melting of a dream."

And now Aeneas saw at the far end of the valley apart, a bushy wood loud with the forest's rustling sounds; and saw Lethe's River, where it flows before the Homes of Peace. About this river like bees in a meadow on a fine day, settling on flowers of every kind, when lilies gleaming white are sprinkled everywhere and all the fields are noisy with the hum, the souls of countless tribes and nations were flitting. Aeneas was startled by the sudden sight and in his bewilderment wished to have his doubts explained and find what might this river be, that he saw before him, and they who crowded its banks with numerous array. His father Anchises gave answer, "They are Souls who are destined to live in the body a second time and at Lethe's wave they are drinking the waters which abolish care and give enduring release from memory. I have long desired to tell you of them and point them out to you in person for you to see; I wished to detail them to you, these descendants of my line, that you might rejoice with me the more, for having found Italy."

"Oh Father, am I then to believe, that of these souls some go soaring hence, up to the world beneath our sky and return once more into dreary matter?"

"I shall tell you indeed and I shall not leave you in suspense my Son." Anchises took up his tale and revealed each truth in due order.

"Now first the Sky and the Lands, and the watery plains, the Moon's gleaming face, the titanic Sun and the stars are all strengthened by the Spirit working within them, and by Mind, which is blended into all the vast Universe and pervades every part of it, enlivening the whole mass. From Spirit and Mind are created men and beasts; and from Spirit and Mind the flying things and the strange creatures that Ocean beneath its surface brings into being, all have their lives. The strength in their seeds is the strength of fire and their origin is of Heaven; in so far as they are not hampered by the body's evil, nor their perceptions dazed by their members that are of earth, and the parts of them that are imbued with death. The body is the cause of fear and desire, of sorrow and of joy and is the reason why, enclosed within the darkness of their windless prison, they cannot look with wide eyes at free air. And indeed, even when on their last day the light of life departs, all evil and all the ills of the body still do not entirely pass from sad soul, for it cannot but be that some of the engrafted faults have long been hardening within, growing inveterate. Accordingly, souls are ceaselessly schooled by retribution, and pay in punishment for their old offences. Some are hung stretched and helpless, for the winds to blow upon them. For others the persuasive wickedness is washed away in an enormous gulf, or is burnt out of them by fire. Each of us finds the world of death fitted unto himself. Then afterwards we are released to wander freely about wide Elysium, and we possess the Fields of Joy, until length of days, as time's cycle is completed, has removed the hardened corruption, and leaves without taint now, a perception pure and bright, a spark of elemental fire. Now when these souls have trodden the full cycle of a thousand years. God calls all of them forth in long procession to Lethe's River, and this he does so that when they again visit the sky's vault, they may be without memory, and a wish to re-enter bodily life may dawn."

Anchises finished and now he led his son and the Sibyl into the midst of a great gathering of souls, who were all busy in conversation. So did they wander everywhere about that land, in the

broad plain's bright haze, reviewing all things there. There are
the Twin Gates of Sleep, of which one is said to be of horn,
allowing an easy exit for shadows that are true. The other is all
of shining white Ivory, perfectly made, but the Spirit sends visions
that are false in the light of day. And Anchises having said his
say escorted his Son and the Sibyl with him on their way, and let
them depart through the Gate of Ivory.[12]

This excerpt from Vergil's *Aeneid* not only gives a perfect
exposition of the Orphic Underworld, but stripped of its poetic
allusions, guided Keith and myself in our identification of the
Oracle at Baiae.

This description reflects the Orphic belief in the nature of
Paradise. We see that their ideal was a perfected continuation
of the joys of life on earth.

If there was thought to be anything parallel to the Christian
Heaven and Community of Saints worshipping God, there is
no reference to it to be found in Orphic writings. The final resting place, The Isles of the Blest, were clearly only a greater
perfection of the Elysian Fields, "Where the Sun never sets and
always gentle zephyrs blow".

The Orphic Underworld was a direct evolution from the
Homeric. It was not contaminated with any oriental metaphysical considerations. The inhabitants are truly 'earthy', and many
of the concepts recall the myths of the pre-Hellenic Gods. Zeus
the Olympian took over from a very ancient and firmly established cult in Crete, the god Zagraeus; giving himself the title
of Zeus-Zagraeus. In order to strengthen his position in relation
to the old cult the myth was created that Olympian Zeus, born
in the Peloponnesus on the mainland of Greece, spent his in-
fancy in Crete protected by the Curetes. These Curetes formed
part of the attendants upon the old Mountain God of Crete. In
the same way at the very ancient sanctuary of the Kabeiri at
Thebes in Boeotia (Greece) pictures show two figures, an old
man seated, holding a wine cup in his hand and in front of him
stands a child. On a vase with this scene upon it, women are
offering playthings to the child, who is clearly the more important of the two figures. All the figures in the scene are named,
the seated man is Kabeiri, and the child simply *pais* (the Greek
word for child). Elsewhere these same two are labelled Zeus
and Dionysius. The Sanctuary at Thebes was excavated many

years ago and yielded much evidence to show that the Orphic Mysteries were performed there.

The Kabeiri and child are an intriguing parallel to Christianity of the Son of God with no Mother. It is one of the strange things about the Greek religion, that they never conceived the idea of the trinity. I think the reason can be found in the fact that Hera, the spouse of Zeus, had been the original Goddess. The Olympic priests found it quite impossible to suppress her worship, so they incorporated her into their Pantheon, as the wife of Zeus. In spite of differing opinions, it can be shown with some authority, that the children she is supposed to have had by Zeus, were already in existence in pre-Hellenic times under other names. Hera was Virgin Goddess and her children were produced parthenogenetically, by touching flowers and by other miraculous means.

An Orphic initiation probably took the form of reading from the Orphic Rhapsodies and the singing of choral hymns. The initiate was dressed in a white linen tunic bound with white ribbons and he held the Thyrsus in his hand. The Thyrsus was a wand made from a reed at the top of which was a fir cone bound with tendrils of ivy. The fir cone had magical properties, as it was used to sprinkle holy water on the celebrants to exorcise any evil spirits. Some kind of dance was performed "in slow measured step". Finally the initiate was given a homily by the officiating Elder, as to the precepts he must follow to attain perfection and salvation of his soul from eternal oblivion. These include abstinence from meat and certain other foods, such as beans; taking of any form of life was prohibited and so was the wearing of wool, which deprived the sheep of his winter coat. The initiate doubtless inspected the contents of the Sacred Chest, which was carried in their processions. This contained, according to Clement of Alexandria, a Christian writer of the first century A.D., a serpent, spinning tops, an apple, knuckle bones, a flock of wool, and other items of a similar nature. Whether these had each and severally, some Orphic significance, or whether the collection was just a reminder of the toys that had been used by the Titans, to distract the attention of the child, whilst they killed him, is a constant theme of discussion amongst students of Orphism.

When we come to seek the resemblance to Christianity inherent in the tenets of Orpheus, we must bear in mind, that Christianity today is a very different conception from that of the first century A.D. The early Christians, like all other people of that time, were profoundly impressed by the teachings and legends of Orpheus. Portraits and allegorical pictures of Orpheus appear freely in the Roman Christian catacombs. The Jews had adopted Orpheus as the parallel of David, the "Musician who could charm the beasts of the Field and raise Hosannas to God". Pictures show Orpheus as the Good Shepherd, carrying the Lost Lamb on his shoulder and as such he was adopted by the early Christians. In the formative days of Christianity many Pagan practices were adopted to assist in conversion. There was also the need for not attracting too much attention to the Church, as the religion was proscribed by the authorities. Many pagan rites were used as symbols in this way, which would be well understood by the initiated. Guthrie quotes "I am the true vine", as a saying of Jesus, using the Dionysian rites. One very interesting seal or charm, now in the Berlin Museum, has aroused a deal of discussion. The seal dates from the fourth century A.D., and depicts the crucifixion of a man on a Christian cross. The wording on the seal reads "Orpheus Bakkikos"; above his head are the stars, seven in number, and the crescent moon; the base of the cross stands in a vee, doubtless representing the earth. The great German authority on Orpheus, Dr. Eisler, maintains that Orpheus was indeed crucified and that the Christians took the crucifixion from Orphism. He cites in support of this that it was not until the fifth century A.D. that Christian representation of the Crucifixion began to appear. However this may be, it all demonstrates the great influence of Orpheus. So great . . . that the apologists realised the close similarity between the Orphic and the Christian tenets and issued angry warnings against their acceptance.

Guthrie after remarking that "religious ideas are never the same from one century to another" goes on to point out some of the striking resemblances between Orphism and Christianity. "Both Christ and Dionysius are Sons of God, and both died and suffered and were resurrected. But why choose the Orphic Dionysius for comparison with Jesus on these points? They are commonplaces of the gods of the decline of paganism. They are true of Osiris and Adonis and many another god, who were

at least as well known in the Graeco-Roman world as the
Orphic Dionysius, if not better. If there is borrowing by Christianity here, it is from the general religious atmosphere of the
age, not from the Orphics. And it is true—it was inevitable—
that this atmosphere in their surroundings did have an effect
on the early Christians when their dogmas were hardening and
setting. The process went on in the succeeding centuries until
almost all the paganism of the world into which Jesus was born,
has crept back into his religion, and is to be found in some
part or other of the world and especially of the Mediterranean.
It is a process which was started by Paul who was the Preacher
above all to the Greeks, and whose Hellenism doubtless contributed to his success with them."

The sacrifice of Jesus was a voluntary self-sacrifice, and this
is a purely Christian concept, all pagan gods being virtually
murdered in their rituals. The Christian Sacrament of eating
their God resembles the pagan communion. But it seems doubtful if, when this rite was first instituted, it was intended to be
more than a symbol of unity. The present day mystic symbolism was a later addition.

It was unquestionably in the conception of the Underworld
and the judgement of souls with punishments and rewards,
where Orphism assisted in the formulation of the Christian
Purgatory. But Orphism was solely concerned with the individual and this was the great difference, as the Christians held
together as a group and were quick to help one another in
adversity or need.

The fearful punishments in Hades depicted in the great painting at Delphi, inspired many artists who decorated the red-
black and other painted vases. These offered an irresistible
temptation to the proselytes of an intolerant religion, like
Christianity, to intimidate their converts into strict obedience
of the directions of the priests. The early Chrstian Fathers
exceeded even the Greek pagans in devising new terrors for the
wicked and heretical. Bearing in mind the times and the tendency of the simple-minded people to believe anything that was
put to them in the 'Name of God', it is probable that here we
have the secret of the fearful power of the priests and the reason
for the final conquest and destruction of the Roman Empire
by the Church.

Entrance (*left*) to the Great Antrum. This is immediately below the aperture shown in the preceding picture. The awe-inspiring portal to Hades (*right*) is well shown in this picture, taken from the floor on the entrance to tunnel 270.

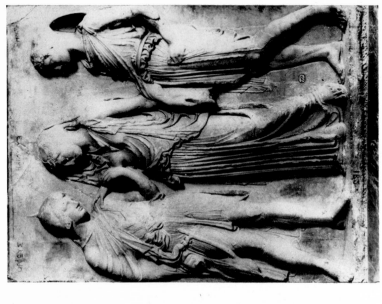

Colin Hardie standing in the Original Entrance (*left*). Maybe this entrance was in use before the Temple was built. Orpheus, Eurydice and Hermes (*right*). Photo of a bas-relief in Naples Museum.

Orphism was cradled in Athens and in Italy, and by the time of the Roman annexation of Magna Grecia, it must have been a very strong religious force which contributed materially to the synthesis of the Church at Rome, through its contacts with the pagan cults at Baiae and generally in the Naples area.

There were no Orphic temples for the simple reason that a person could be an Orphic and still worship any number of other gods.

Orphism was a way of life which achieved its results by example. Orpheus succeeded in abolishing cannibalism from Greece, and in taming the wild rites of Dionysius into something more decorous. He influenced men like Onomacritus and Pythagoras in the great days of Classical Greece, to think it worthwhile to codify his ideas, and from the sixth century B.C. onwards Orphism was preparing the Western World for the eventual reception of the Christian religion.

There is nothing today at Baiae to show if the Sanctuary was actually used as an Orphic meeting place. There is an Orphic mosaic floor, to which I refer in Chapter V, but it cannot be older than about A.D. 80. This, and other indications, suggests a strong Orphic cult in the neighbourhood of Baiae in the time of Vergil, but we do not want to give the impression that in our opinion, Orphic rites were performed in the Oracle of the Dead. They may have been, that is all we are prepared to say.

It was a year before we located the shrine, and another year before we could assert with confidence that we had truly identified this gem of religious sites. In fact it is probably the best preserved and amongst the more authentic places of this nature. In spite of its great antiquity, the continuity of its existence until it was buried is well documented, and its disappearance under the vineyards for 2,000 years has saved it from vandalism.

Its civilising influence on the Campania and the Italiote tribes was on a par with that of Delphi in Greece. In later times it seems to have been taken over by Cuma and made one with the Oracle of the Sibyl, which was consulted by Kings of Rome, and even by Bishops of Rome as late as the fourth century A.D., a fact that indicates how long it took the infant Christianity to dispense with pagan assistance. To this day in Southern Italy, many of the rites in the religious processions are still those of

F

the pagan gods with the names changed. Even in St. Peter's, Rome, on Easter Day the Sacred Fire is kindled and all the candles used in the ceremonies lighted from it. This is the Sacred Fire of Hestia and the Hearth that was the centre of Greek life 3,000 years before Christ was born.

NOTES

1. Pausanias, VIII, xxx, 2-5.
2. Diodorus Siculus, sundry references to Orpheus.
3. Apollonius of Rhodes, *Argonautica* 1. 512 *seq.*
4. W. K. C. Guthrie, *Orpheus and the Greek Religion*, p. 13.
5. Sundry ancient sources (fragments).
6. Robert Graves, *The Greek Myths*, Heracles.
7. Diodorus Siculus, V, 79.
8. Diodorus Siculus, III, 62-8.
9. Pausanias, I, xxxvii, 4.
10. Euripides, *The Cretans*, Chorus.
11. W. K. C. Guthrie, *Orpheus and the Greek Religion*, pp. 171 *seq.*
12. Vergil, *Aeneid* VI, *passim.*

3

Search for the Oracle of the Dead

Certain places on the Earth seem to be endowed with a special sanctity, which has been with them since time immemorial. Religions change, new gods are reverenced, but the aura of mystery remains inherent in the site. So with Baiae and the crater of Avernus, which has been revered as the entrance to the Underworld for more than four thousand years. One cannot help being attracted by the legends and myths about the place, preserved for us by ancient writers, poets and historians. I can look out of my window and 'see' these legends all round. To the left is the River of Ocean and the beach where Odysseus landed to consult the Seer Teiresias in the Underworld. To the right is the grim sixteenth-century Spanish fortress, built on the ruins of Julius Caesar's palace. A walk of less than a mile, brings me to the Bay of Baiae, ringed with the ruins of the ancient city.

Here I met with Keith Jones, who was serving in the United States Navy, in the NATO Base at Naples. We began discussing how to get the best satisfaction out of looking at ruins, especially, as in the case of Baiae, when there is no published information and no one seemed to know anything about their history. The obvious answer was to seek the information for ourselves; but where to begin was our problem. The mystery of the crater of Avernus with its dark brown circular lake; the terraces of houses at Baiae and the submerged town all along the shores of the dyke separating Lake Lucrino from the sea; all impinged on the imagination to an irresistible degree. Where to begin? Here we had the answer. Could we solve the problems associated with Avernus and the Underworld? Could we recapture the atmosphere of Roman Baiae, the most luxurious sink of pleasure and iniquity ever to exist? We looked in vain for any traces of such luxury in the poor crumbling walls, here and there in the vineyards. It seemed a bleak prospect, but we decided to try.

As I said above, one cannot help being attracted by the legends and myths about these places preserved for us by the ancient historians. To the modern mind 'myths and legends' convey an impression of unreality. But to the ancient historian they were traditional history, handed down orally from generation to generation. They cannot be dismissed as religious fantasies and poetic dreams. We know today that Maori traditional history has proved reliable over several hundred generations and the Greek myths should receive comparable credence.

A hundred years ago Heinrich Schliemann confounded the pundits, by believing in the accounts of 'legendary events' given by Homer and Pausanias. One well-known archaeologist, Grote, wrote that "the legends were invented by the Greeks out of their inexhaustible imagination to fill in the blanks of their unknown past. To believe that a King called Minos ever existed in Crete, or that the Trojan War had been fought, was actually foolish . . . it was equally foolish to deny the possibility." What happened? Schliemann went to the Dardanelles and dug up Homer's city of Troy under the hill of Hissarlik. Not satisfied with this success, he went to Mycenae and dug up the tombs of the ancient kings. The fact that he thought he had found the tomb of Agamemnon, does not invalidate his faith in the truth of the old legends. This success was followed by an even greater. Sir Arthur Evans bought an amulet from a woman in Athens, inscribed with strange unreadable characters. Intuition led him to think it had originated in Crete. So to Crete he went, and bought the land under which, he believed, was the ancient capital. He then hired help, and in two months had dug up a whole unknown civilisation. King Minos and the Minoans, about whom Thucydides wrote, "Minos is the first ruler we know of who possessed a fleet, and controlled all of what are now Greek waters. He ruled the islands and colonised most of them, setting up his own sons as chiefs." The Minoan Empire lasted for 1,500 years, equal say to the time from the Romans leaving Britain until the present day. Yet until Sir Arthur Evans found Knossos, no one believed in the Minoans' existence. So much has been found to be true of these 'legendary nations' and places, that today a reappraisal is being made. Another outstanding success due to belief in legends, is the recovery of the history of the Hittites. One archaeologist described this as "having achieved the impossible, by deciphering an unknown language, written by an unknown people".

Today, the voyage of Odysseus (Ulysses) is accepted as having taken place. Odysseus was a real person who made one, or more, voyages of discovery round the coasts of Italy and Sicily during the second millenium B.C. His name indicates by its termination -eus, that he was older than the Greeks or Hellenes; so he was probably a Pelasgian, or a Cretan. Homer himself lived in one of the cities of South-west Asia Minor, which were of Cretan colonisation.[1]

In considering myths and legends bearing on ancient religions, one must take into account the fanatical attempts by the Fathers of the Church, who dwelt in Alexandria and in Asia Minor during the first three or four centuries of our era, at suppression of all concepts opposed to the early Christian ideas. On the other hand, in their attempts to belittle the pagan gods, they have preserved for us a wealth of detail of their nature and rites, which otherwise would have been lost to us. We learn that they had access to a vast amount of material that has disappeared. We also learn that the rites in so many instances, were those that they themselves professed; that they found it necessary to adopt the old procedure, merely changing the names. In the mountain villages of Southern Italy, there are scores of instances of this. For example, the moon goddess, Brizo became Santa Brigida, the patroness of all the Arts. She is St. Brigit in Ireland.

The proper place to start an archaeological investigation is not in the field but in the library. We therefore spent several weeks in the Biblioteca Nazionale in Naples, seeking all the references in Greek and Roman authors, which might have a bearing on our problem. Whilst we found that specific references to Baiae were few and far between, there is quite a fund of knowledge available about Magna Grecia, the Italiote tribes and the gradual expansion of Roman power over Southern

Italy. Chance remarks of Tacitus (the Roman historian) like,
"Without further enquiry Claudius sent the Commander of the
Guard, Rufius Crespinus, with enough troops to suppress a
rebellion. Proceeding at full speed, Crespinus found Decimus
Valerius Asiaticus at Baiae and took him to Rome in chains."
His crime was the jealousy of the Empress Messalina, because
Decimus was the lover of Poppaea Sabina. He was tried, con-
demned and forced to commit suicide. Incidents such as these,
show that Baiae was a very important place. Decimus was an
ex-consul, one of many who had a villa there.

Then we saw that Puteoli, Cuma and Baiae with Lucrino and
Bacoli (Bauli) in Roman times, were treated as one comprehensive built-up area. In fact during the last century B.C. and
the first two or three A.D., the Phlegrean Fields were the most
thickly populated area of the Empire outside Rome itself. Baiae
was a hotbed of religious jealousies, spies and seditionists from
all the conquered countries of the Near East. They passed
through the great port of Puteoli, seeking information and
sympathisers amongst the Roman aristocracy, most of whom
were power-hungry self-seekers, always ready to listen to political intrigue. After the conquest of Greece, in 200 B.C. and the
annexation of Magna Grecia, the purely Greek nature of the
Mysteries at Avernus, tended to become Italiote, that is to say,
charged with modernisms introduced by Orphism and by
Samnite and Etruscan thought.

The ruins at Baiae were said, in the local guide book, to be
the Roman Thermae, which history says were the most luxurious in the world. We looked in vain for any trace of this
luxury, and it did not take us long to realise that the terraces
of vaulted houses, had nothing to do with Roman Baiae. At
first we thought that all these buildings represented the 'service'
part of the Thermae, where the slaves lived, where the stores
were kept, and so on. But as both of us are engineers, and we
felt that the Romans were eminently practical men, we knew
the layout was incompatible with a designed service depart-
ment of a great establishment. We noted that although at least
five major reconstructions were traceable, together with innumerable repairs, the general design appeared to have
remained constant over a long period of time.

The place was older than the Roman occupation and was a

typical terraced town of Etruscan or Italiote design, similar to many hundreds of such villages dotted over the hillsides of Southern Italy. Its proximity to Avernus opened up a new line of thought. We began to read all that we could find in the ancient writers about the old belief that Avernus was the entrance to the Underworld. Before long we became convinced that such a tremendous concept must have been supported by shrines and sanctuaries, over a very long period. In fact as time went on during the Pax Romana, all the intellectual activities in the Roman world concentrated on Naples and the Phlegrean Fields. The religious importance of Baiae grew in like measure. The ruins of the town have survived. Was it too much to hope that some trace of the religious activities might also have survived, and could they be found?

We decided that we would explore the whole region systematically. We formulated our plans on the writings of Homer, Ephorus, Strabo and Vergil. The next two years were spent in exploring every hole in the ground within three miles of Avernus. But first we had to learn all about the myths and legends of the Underworld, and decide how much was poetic fantasy and how much offered clues for the finding of possible relics.

Homer lived about 800 B.C., in one of the cities along the coast of Asia Minor. He wrote the *Odyssey*, which everyone still reads and enjoys, the tale of the voyage of Odysseus, his amorous adventures with Circe and Calypso, and the skilful manner in which he alone escapes all the frightful dangers of the unknown seas. Today, this is considered a true account of a voyage by an historic personage round the coasts of Sicily and western Italy. When considered impartially, such stories as those of Scylla and Charybdis are no more fantastic than those brought back by the mariners of the sixteenth century about their voyages to Cathay and the Indies, telling of the Mermaids and Sea Serpents of the Sargasso Sea and the Southern Ocean where the Flying Dutchman sails for ever in his ghost ship.

It was perfectly normal for Odysseus to wish to consult a Seer, before setting out on his journey home. No undertaking was ever begun in ancient times, until the omens were favourable. In the case of a sea voyage the most stringent efforts were made to ensure a safe arrival. Before starting, sacrifice was

made to the god of the desired wind and the captain made
certain that the sacrifice had been favourably received by the
gods. Then during the voyage, offerings were continuously
made to the gods of the sea; on occasion of a great storm even
human sacrifices were made. Remember the story of Jonah,
who was thrown into the sea to appease the storm-god, but was
saved by being swallowed by a whale.[2]

Circe tells Odysseus,

Don't think of lingering on shore for lack of a pilot. Set up your
mast, spread the white sail and sit down in the ship. The North
Wind will blow her on her way and when she has brought you
across the River of Ocean, you will come to a wild coast and to
Persephone's Grove, where the tall poplars grow and the willows
that so quickly shed their seeds. Beach your boat there by Ocean's
swirling Stream and march on into Hades' Kingdom of Decay.
There, the River of Fire and the River of Lamentation, which is
a branch of the River Styx, unite round a pinnacle of rock, to
pour their thundering streams into Acheron. This is the spot, My
Lord, that I bid you seek out.[3]

Odysseus relates:

A friendly breeze sprang up from astern, and filled the sail of our
blue-prowed ship. All we had to do, after putting the tackle in
order fore and aft was to sit still, while the wind and the helms-
man kept her straight. With a taut sail, she forged all day till the
sun went down and left her to pick her way through the night.

Thus she brought us to the deep-flowing River of Ocean and
the frontiers of the world, where the fog-bound Cimmerians live
in the City of Perpetual Mist. When the bright Sun climbs to the
sky and puts the stars to flight, no ray from him can penetrate to
them, nor can he see them, as he drops from Heaven and sinks
once more to Earth. For dreadful Night has spread her mantle
over that unhappy folk.

Here we beached our boat and after disembarking the sheep,
made our way along the banks of the River of Ocean, until we
reached the spot that Circe had described.[4]

The River of Ocean was the Strait between the Island of
Prochida and the mainland. In 1000 B.C., the volcanic activity
of the Phlegrean Fields was very much greater than it is now.
Although today there are but two or three hot springs at Baiae,
in former times the Bay probably had the appearance of

Rotorua, or the Yellowstone National Park, where hot springs and steaming geysers fill the air with mist and the smell of sulphur. No wonder it was called the Bay of Perpetual Mist. The Cimmerians were already there, or Homer, living in far-off Asia Minor, could not have heard of their existence. Mention of them is proof that, either the voyage of Odysseus had actually taken place and he was a real person, or Homer must have been told about them by another sea captain who had been to Baiae.

Confirmation of the existence of the Cimmerians is to be found in the writings of Strabo, where he devotes several pages to Avernus. He says,

The people prior to my time, were wont to make Avernus the setting of the fabulous story of the *Necyia* (*The Odyssey*); and what is more writers tell us that there was, actually, an Oracle of the Dead there, and that Odysseus visited it . . . and the natives used to add the further fable, that all birds that fly over it fall down into the water, being killed by the vapours that rise from it, as is the case with all Plutonia. And the people used to suppose, that this too was a Plutonian place and that the Cimmerians had actually been there. At any rate, only those who had actually sacrificed beforehand and propitiated the Nether Deities could sail into Avernus, and the priests who held the locality on lease were there to give directions in all such matters; and there is a fountain of potable water at this place; but people used to abstain from it, because they regarded it as the water of the River Styx; and the Oracle too is situated somewhere near it; and further the hot springs nearby and Lake Acherusia betokened the River Pyriphlegethon. Again Ephorus, in the passage where he claims the locality in question for the Cimmerians, says; they live in Underground houses which they call *argillae* and it is through tunnels that they visit one another back and forth; and they live on what they can get from Mining [Divining?], and from those who consult the Oracle, which is situated far beneath the Earth.

And those who live about the Oracle, have an ancestral custom that no one should see the Sun, but should go outside the caverns only at night; and it is for this reason that the poet [Homer] speaks of them as follows, "And never does the shining sun look upon them." But later the Cimmerians were destroyed by a certain king, because the response of the Oracle did not turn out in his favour. The seat of the Oracle, however still endures, although it has been removed to another place.

Such are the stories that the people before my time used to tell, but now that the forest round Avernus has been cut down by Agrippa, and the tracts of land have been built up with houses, all these stories have proven to be mere myths. And yet the Cocceius who made not only the tunnel [that connects with Cuma], but also the one from Dicaearchia to Neapolis [The Crypta Napolitana], was pretty well acquainted with the story just now related about the Cimmerians, and it may very well be that he also deemed it an ancestral custom for this region that its roads should run through tunnels.[5]

These two extracts were the bases upon which, we decided, that there had been an Oracle of the Dead at or near Avernus. It had been there in 1000 B.C. when Homer wrote about it, and it was still there in 500 B.C., in the time of Ephorus. Strabo writing about 20 B.C. says it was destroyed by Agrippa, that is to say in 40-30 B.C., but it was probably reinstated in some form by Augustus when peace returned.[6]

Keith and I felt that the only way to make sure we did not miss any attributes of the Underworld beliefs, or of the *Aeneid* story was to begin our search at Cuma.

The Oracle of the Sibyl had been known to have been operating as late as the fourth century A.D., but like the Oracle of the Dead at Avernus, the site was lost and forgotten. Amadeo Maiuri following the clue given in the *Aeneid* by Vergil,

> Then Aeneas climbed the rocky hill
> Where, on the crest the Temple of Apollo stands
> And there the fearsome cavern of the
> Awesome Sibyl lies, whence came her prophesies
> Inspired by Great Delius, himself,

excavated the famous Antrum in 1932. It is, indeed, a fearsome cavern 150 yards long with the ancient Mycenean Axe-head section. Aligned exactly north and south with the *Cella* of the Sibyl at the southern end, it conforms in a truly eerie manner with the description given by Vergil. Here, Aeneas came to consult his father in the Underworld. He was informed by the priests of the temple that the Sibyl would assist him in his desire, if he complied with the rites and sacrifices that such a tremendous project required. After the funeral of Misenus, the Sibyl conducted Aeneas to a place where there was another 'fearful cavern', down which she would guide him to the Underworld. Cuma stands isolated from the crater of Avernus, by a wide stretch of what was then, probably, marshy jungle. We noted that at Cuma itself there is nothing that suggests an Entrance to the Underworld, nothing with any connection with the Avernus beliefs. There was also the evidence of the voyage of Odysseus, in which he by-passed Cuma on his way to the Oracle. We therefore rejected Cuma as the site of the Oracle of the Dead. In order to reach the spot where he beached his ship, he was directed by Circe to sail his ship through the River of Ocean, land and proceed on foot to the Oracle. In order to do this he must have sailed right past Cuma, as the River of Ocean is the Strait between the Island of Prochida and the mainland. In fact, Cuma is not mentioned by Homer in the *Odyssey*. The probable reason was, that Cuma had been founded by explorers from the Trojan area of Asia Minor, so Odysseus being an enemy would never have entered their City. The fact that he beached his ship in the bay that is now the Lago di Miseno, adds to the burden of proof, that the Oracle was not to be found at Cuma.

So after examining all the tunnels at Cuma, we went to Avernus itself.

Two or three miles south of Cuma, is another similar isolated hill, known today as the Monte di Prochida. Between this and Cuma is Lake Fusaro, which was known to the ancients as the Marsh of Acherusia, into which flowed the Rivers of Hell. On the east shore, about half way along, is to be seen a boiling water spring which the men of old called the River Acheron, a tributary of the River Styx. Incidentally this hot spring is in a building of Neronian date and probably formed part of the villa of Seneca. Seneca was a famous Roman, who was born in Spain, came to Italy and got involved with Messalina. He was exiled for eight years, but returned to become the confidant of Nero and possible originator of the scheme to murder Nero's mother, Agrippina.

We made a thorough survey of the crater of Avernus. Here, we felt that topographical and volcanic changes, might have so obscured the ancient scene, that all traces would have been destroyed. Ephorus had stated that the Oracle was removed from its original site, owing to the unfavourable reply it had given to the enquiry of the ruler of the region. Eponomeo had last erupted in 500 B.C. accompanied by a great earthquake that had caused widespread damage that extended to the mainland where it had spread 'havoc and panic'. Maybe, at this time the topography was changed. It could well have been that to suggest the Entrance to the Underworld, there was originally a crater lake with a small island in the centre. Did this disappear when Eponomeo erupted for the last time? Then there is the proximity of Monte Nuovo, immediately to the east, in fact rising in the gap of the crater wall of Avernus. Today the depth of the Avernus crater lake, is said to be nearly 200 feet in the centre. Why was it not completely filled up by the eruption of Monte Nuovo? This is a very interesting point. Monte Nuovo was erupted to a height of 450 feet in the course of two terrible days in 1538. But the explosive force does not seem to have been able to do more than deposit a cone of ashes, immediately around the crater, the floor of which is practically at sea level. There was no dust or ash blown over the countryside, as happened in the famous eruption of Vesuvius, when so many towns were buried. This, then, may account for the fact that Avernus retains the shape and appearance that it had in 500 B.C. In spite also of changes of land level due to the movements of bradyseism both at Baiae and at Pozzuoli, the level of Lake Avernus is still the same as it was in the time of Agrippa (30 B.C.), as the holes in the marble quays, to which the Roman warships were moored, are still there and at their correct level above the water. This shows that the craters in the sea off Baiae and Pozzuoli are quite distinct from that of Avernus.

The crater wall of Avernus is very steep inside, but it slopes gradually on the outside, merging into the long ridge, forming the backbone of the little promontory or peninsula of Bacoli-Misenum. The Bay of Baiae is a subsidiary crater in the wall of Avernus.

The appearance of the countryside today, is that of intensely cultivated fields and terraces of vineyards covering all the slopes, hills and craters. It is difficult to visualise that until a couple of hundred years ago all was impenetrable forest teeming with wild animals. This would account for the complete absence of Roman remains, except at certain well specified points. Cuma and Baiae must have enjoyed almost complete isolation from the rest of the Campania until around 400 B.C., when the Oscans succeeded in subduing Cuma. There they remained until the coming of the Romans a hundred years later.

We found there are no Greek or pre-Hellenic remains inside the crater of Avernus, but there were many traces of Agrippa's dockyards. There are ruins of a large Thermal Establishment in the north-eastern quadrant, standing on a wide flat quay, which at one time, clearly extended round the whole circumference of the lake. In spite of the eruption of Monte Nuovo, the general appearance must be very like that of 44 B.C. when Agrippa began to build the dockyards in place of the Shrines of Apollo. The water level is still the same. There are two tunnels, which are cut through the crater wall. There is evidence that they are both of the same date, and were a part of the dockyard complex. The western one runs from the lake level to Cuma; it is the one mentioned by Strabo as having been built by Cocceius. The gallery is about a mile long, ten or twelve feet wide, by ten feet high and lit by lamp niches. Its purpose was to provide a means of communication with the garrison at Cuma and also to the beach at Cuma.[7] This, to my mind, suggests two things. The forest was, to all intents and purposes, still impassable and the inner wall of the crater of Avernus so steep, that the only practical way into the lake, is by the breach in the wall on the eastern side. Doubtless there was the further consideration that ships coming down from Rome (the port of Antium) could find shelter to discharge passengers and cargo at Liternum (three miles north of Cuma) and thus save some fifteen to twenty miles of sea journey in case of bad weather. The tunnel also completed the strategic defence of the peninsula extending to Misenum.

The second tunnel is, from our point of view, the more important. For over fifty years it has been called the Grotto della Sibilla. The custodian Signor Alessandro, maintains that it is the original entrance to the Underworld. Before describing the investigation that Keith and I made, I will quote from the official Italian guide book *The Phlegrean Fields* by Professor A. Maiuri.

A very ancient Oracle of the cult of the Dead at the Gates of Avernus, the presence of a hot spring, in which popular legend saw the River Styx, have maintained for the crater of Avernus, through the centuries, its sacred character of consecration to the gods of the Underworld. Even Hannibal, when he sacked the Cuma region in 209 B.C., felt the urge to perform sacrificial rites to the powerful and mysterious deities of the place. Not even the great transformation carried out by Agrippa could eradicate the sense of religious terror, that the very nature of the crater inspires. When, with the triumph of Christianity, the cult of the Oracle of the Sibyl at Cuma ceased, and even the Roman Empire lost its vital force, the area fell into decay and was abandoned to silence and mystery. The great tunnels of communication, which the Romans had made under the hills fell in, slowly filling up with water. Popular legend again took possession and connected the tunnels with the Oracle and transferred the Sibyl to Avernus.

On the west side of the crater, about 300 yards from the house of the custodian (on the road at the entrance to the crater), a path through the chestnut woods leads to the so-called Grotta della Sibilla. It is a gallery about 200 yards long, 12 feet wide by 12 feet high (in places a little higher) which traverses the hill in a perfectly straight line, east and west, to connect the Lake of Avernus with that of Lucrino. There are no light shafts, but owing to its short length, it seems to have had sufficient natural light to serve its purpose. At the western end, there is a rectangular vestibule, lined with *opus reticulatum*. At the eastern end just before reaching the opening there is a rough passage and stair, leading down to a series of chambers, now partly filled with water, due to bradyseism, which local tradition would like to call the Bath of the Sibyl. The gallery like those of the other *Crypta* of Cuma and Naples, cut in the tufa with characteristic Roman precision, are nothing more than passages created for the direct communication between Lucrino and Avernus and Cuma, and it is more than likely that they formed a part of the extensive programmes of military works carried out by Agrippa about the year 37 B.C. In addition to the navigation canal connecting the sea with the lake, it was necessary to have shore communication, both for the crews and for the dockyard workers and also for greater security in case of trouble at the outer moles at Lucrino.[8]

Keith and I made an extensive survey of the Lucrino end of the Grotta. Here the tunnel exit comprises a series of important chambers, connected with wide stairways. The only excavation, so far carried out, has exposed part of the construction on the left, or south side of the entrance. Holes in the brickwork permit of partial inspection of the work on the right of the entrance and it seems certain that here also are chambers waiting to be excavated. On the left, one flight of the main stair zig-zags upwards to unknown heights; the corresponding flight leads down to a series of chambers some twenty feet below the level of the tunnel. There is about four feet of water on the floor of the rooms, but otherwise there is nothing remarkable about them. They have every appearance of a 'guardroom', for the soldiers controlling transit through the Grotta. All the masonry is Roman brickwork and there is nothing to suggest a religious significance. There is certainly nothing to recall anything in the *Aeneid*. We also were convinced that the so-called Grotta della Sibilla is merely the 'Workmen's Entrance' to Agrippa's dockyard.

Before dismissing Avernus as a possible site for the Oracle, we also examined all the holes in the cliff face above the Lucrino entrance to the Grotta della Sibilla, round to Punta del'Epitaffio (the northern arm of the Bay of Baiae). There has been a good deal of damage by landslide and cliff falls, but enough traces remain, to prove, that here must have been a well populated area in the time of Roman Baiae. Recalling that, at that time, Lake Lucrino extended as far as Puteoli, some two miles to the east, and also some two miles inland, the view must have been impressive. From the Punta del'Epitaffio to Puteoli, the sandy strip, half a mile wide forming the dyke to Lake Lucrino was covered with the beautiful beach houses of the Romans. The lake was filled with the Roman fleet, with all the associated military activity on the esplanade below the cliff. Doubtless the villas on the cliff-top were those of Agrippa and his officers.

None of the tunnel entrances proved useful to us. They were mostly water conduits or Roman drainage ducts.

The Ridge, being the outside wall of the crater of Avernus, still retains its volcanic fires. Twelve years ago a sudden inburst of boiling water killed all the fish in Lake Lucrino. Towards the Punta del'Epitaffio, the hillside is honeycombed with cave dwellings, still occupied by modern troglodytes. These cave dwellings are supposed locally to have been part of a Thermal Baths erected by Nero, but there does not seem to be much evidence to support this idea. Keith and I were shown round one dwelling by the owner, a happy woman, very proud of the fine rooms they have made. Accompanied by the lady and four or five small children, we went through a series of very hot rooms until we came to a barrier and could go no farther. We noticed, however, that the family dog passed through the barrier and although he did not return with us, he was there, in the outer room when we got there. The whole hillside is probably a maze of galleries.

Punta del'Epitaffio forms the north point of the Bay of Baiae. Upon it stand the crumbling walls of the Temple of Venus Lucrina. From here round the bay to the entrance to the excavations of the "Thermae di Baiae" is perhaps, three-quarters of a mile.[9] It is obvious that the whole hillside is covered with the ruins of houses, or villas similar to those already brought to light in the excavations. In Roman times the population of Baiae was four times that of Naples.

At this stage we began to feel that the ravages of time and the vandalism of man, had probably destroyed all traces of the Oracle. The unstable nature of the ground, the eruption of Monte Nuovo[10], coverage by falls of volcanic dust, and the march of time and the rapacity of 'collectors' had swallowed everything.

Somehow, we had never thought that within the excavations at Baiae was the secret. We naturally assumed that when the ruins were excavated, all the tunnels and entries into the hillside had been explored and their significance noted.

Were the pundits correct, and the whole story of the Entrance to the Underworld and the Oracle of the Dead, merely an invention of Homer and Vergil, with no physical foundation whatsoever?

We did not believe it.

The statements of Ephorus were too convincing, the ancient world knew that there was an Oracle here and this knowledge endured for 2,000 years. We argued the problem afresh and analysed our results so far. The necessary conditions to permit the functioning of such an Oracle with its world-wide appeal called for considerable organisation. This in turn meant a monastery for the priests, housing for the lay-workers round the Oracle, lodging for the pilgrims, lodging for the suppliers of sacrificial animals, byres, food shops and the rest. Where around Avernus were such facilities to be found? Puteoli,

(*Left*) The Dividing of the Ways (looking east into tunnel 270), 400 feet underground. Here the road to Hades divides into three, and the wall blocking the divisions can be clearly seen.

(*Right*) Beginning of the Stair to the Styx in tunnel 290. Robert Love looking at the tiles in the roof marking the former Entrance to Tartarus.

The north and east "doors" of the Inner Sanctuary, blocked by the Romans, after filling the interior entirely with earth brought in from outside.

Baiae and Cuma are the only towns capable of supporting such an activity. There are no mentions of any others in the immediate neighbourhood of Avernus by any ancient writer, nor ruins of any to be seen today. The Oracle had been in existence 500 years before Puteoli was founded, therefore Pozzuoli was automatically excluded.

We found ourselves left with Baiae as the only possible site. From this moment on, every move we made seemed to bring us nearer to success; but success remained elusive for another eighteen months.

Fortunately the custodians had been there when the excavations were carried out and we were able to get first-hand accounts of what they had found before any restoration was carried out.

The entrance to the excavations is at the top of the Sella di Baia, where the road crosses the ridge on its way to Cuma, about ninety feet above sea level. From this point, the ridge runs south for about 400 yards, where it makes a slight bend towards the south-east. In this bend, at some time in the past, a landslide has occurred, burying the ruins lying on a solid platform 75 feet above sea level. Fig. 3 shows the layout of this part of the excavations. The chief custodian, Guido D'Aiuto, told us that this platform was real solid ground. It had never been built on, or in, other than with those buildings that were still there. The terraces of the 'houses' are orientated to conform to the curve of the ridge, and the ruins group themselves naturally into four sections, built at different dates. (A full description of the layout will be found in the official guide book *The Phlegrean Fields* and it is not necessary to repeat it here.)

We come to Section IV however, and note that the ruins on the little platform at the 75-foot level have a different orientation from the rest of the section. Not only this, but the buildings themselves, are different. The remaining main construction of the section can be referred to an epoch round A.D. 80, modified by reconstruction and restoration in the sixteenth century, when the Thermae enjoyed a brief revival as a curative spa.

We are interested in the buildings on the solid platform. The most striking feature, is that they form a specialised group, orientated on a bearing of 330 degrees.[11] Except for a few superimposed cyclopean blocks, forming the wall footings to

G

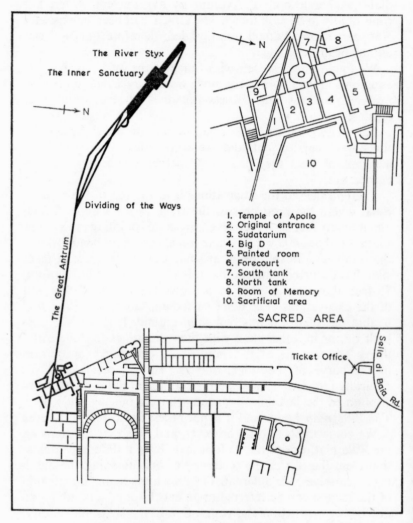

The River Styx

The Inner Sanctuary

→ N

Dividing of the Ways

The Great Antrum

→ N

7   8

9   5

1 2 3 4

10

1. Temple of Apollo
2. Original entrance
3. Sudatarium
4. Big D
5. Painted room
6. Forecourt
7. South tank
8. North tank
9. Room of Memory
10. Sacrificial area

SACRED AREA

Ticket Office

Sella di Baia Rd.

Fig. 3. THE SACRED AREA AT BAIA

the building at the southern end of the group, little is left except the silhouettes of the vaulted ends on the cliff face.

In order to assist the reader in maintaining continuity in the story, I must anticipate to the extent of using the names that we gave to the various buildings and tunnels, after our discovery and identification of the Oracle. Referring again to Fig. 3 "The Sacred Area", we noticed that the tunnel entrances were all confined to the area between the main stair (which is parallel to the Cimmerian stair, separated from it only by a wall) at the southern end of the "Ambulatorium" and the Sacred Area. The whole of the upper part of Section III, has many tunnels and underground chambers, which at first sight, seem to serve no appreciable purpose; until the remarks by Ephorus are recalled. Then the picture clicks into focus. "They live in underground houses which they call *argillae*, and it is through tunnels that they visit each other, back and forth."

Here is the monastery of the Cimmerians. The mystery of their way of life is explainable. They were the priests of the Oracle serving the Dead and darkness of the Underworld. They had a rule, that they never went outside the tunnels, until after sunset and before the dawn. The fact that such a life would mean an early death would count for nothing in those cruel times. As soon as we realised this, we began to explore each tunnel in turn. They have certain characteristics in common. All of them are walk-ways of ample dimensions, about six or seven feet high and more than four feet wide. Within a short distance, never exceeding 60 feet, they end in a vaulted room. In some cases there were subsidiary tunnels from these vaulted rooms, connecting with similar chambers. These are the *argillae* of the Cimmerians.

In order to appreciate the state of the ruins at Baiae, a visual examination is necessary to see the extensive reconstructions and countless repairs, clearly as the result of earthquake damage. In the peaceful appearance of the Phlegrean Fields today, it is difficult to recapture the picture of the instability of the earth's crust in the times we are considering. Pliny the Younger wrote a letter to his friend Tacitus, the historian, describing the great eruption of Vesuvius in A.D. 79. In the course of the letter he says, "for several days [before the eruption], as a preliminary, there were earthquake shocks, but we did not pay much attention, as in the Campania they are very frequent."[12] I have said, there are signs of at least five heavy damages, that called for re-building. But apart from these, Section III, with its theatre, was designed and constructed as a unit. In the process the tunnels and *argillae* of the Cimmerians were converted into cisterns and conduits to feed the fountains lower down on the floor of the bay. But in the upper part, some of the *argillae* were preserved.

In dealing with a conception which was originally Greek, such as the Oracle of the Dead and the cults of Avernus, one tends to overlook the fact that the Romans took over Magna Grecia in 334 B.C., and that for 400 years the Sanctuary at Baiae was in a Roman town. No wonder that there remain no traces of Greek work, except the cyclopean blocks of the temple walls. Nothing remains of the original surface buildings, except the ground plan. Underground, as we shall see later, much of the original Oracle is in a remarkable state of preservation.

It is no longer possible to reconstruct the monastery of the Cimmerians, but it is possible to obtain a general impression of the layout. Parallel with the main stair on the north side of Section III, there is another, cut in the living rock. It commences at the level of the piscina, and ends alongside the "Chapel" of Sosandra, a total rise of about sixty feet. On the south side of this stair are a series of rooms, or *argillae* each some 20 feet by 10 feet, and 10 feet high, one on each terrace level. Further to the south, under the theatre, there are more *argillae*, which doubtless were originally connected to those which have survived intact. The complex extended under the whole of Section III from the piscina to above the chapel of Sosandra. There was total floor space of some one hundred feet square, divided into many *argillae*. These considerable dimensions are not really surprising, when the duties performed by the priests are considered.

They had the morning and the evening sacrifices to carry out, the sacred fires to attend to, temple services with torchlight processions and intercessions to the god. They interpreted dreams and gave omens to all enquirers about to start on a journey or undertake some new project. The sick and the injured all came for medical attention. There were the day to day household chores, the sweeping and cleaning of the temple and the Oracle, the filling of the lamps with oil, repairs to buildings and so on and so on. It is easy to see that perhaps a couple of hundred priests, layworkers and slaves were quartered in the *argillae*.

We talked with the custodian and got him to show us the three rooms under Sosandra, which are illuminated and open to the public. Like all the remainder of the *argillae*, these were converted by the Romans to other uses when Section III was built. But they still give the impression of having been used by a religious community. One especially, is fitted with statue niches, and is decorated with stucco and painted walls. All these rooms were much reduced in size at the reconstruction, as all the walls ring hollow when struck, showing there is hollow space behind. Entry is from the rock-hewn stairway mentioned previously, at a point some eleven feet below ground. For the first few feet the tunnel is lined with masonry, then it is cut in the solid rock. At this point, a glance back reveals that here was a former entrance by stairway from above. The passage is at least four feet wide and more than six feet high. After traversing some forty feet, the passage ends in the centre one, of three chambers. This is a room 10 feet square by 10 feet high. It is lined with stucco-covered tufa masonry and painted, dark red below and white above. In the west wall, in the bottom right hand corner is a hole leading to a small room at the rear some 6 feet square. In the west wall of this, high up in the north corner, is a tunnel which runs westwards for an unknown distance as it is blocked by earth. Returning to the central chamber we see high up in the north corner another tunnel which has been explored for 150 feet to where it is blocked by an earth fall. There is yet another tunnel in these three rooms, which is reached by a hole in the roof of the entry tunnel and extends towards the west to end under the southern of the two vaulted buildings standing upon the 110-foot terrace level. From here it continues to finish at the bottom of a vertical shaft fitted with foot rests, coming up to daylight in the plinth of the temple of the Dioscuri 20 feet higher up the hillside.

To the right and left of the central chamber, are rooms separated from the chamber, by only the thickness of the wall. The one on the south side, was converted into a circular sudatorium, with the usual hypocaust floor, heated by gas from a tunnel visible underneath, but whose further direction cannot be traced. The room to the north has been reduced in size and given a cruciform plan. In the walls are statue niches. Who knows if this was not a meeting place for the early Christians.

I would constantly remind readers, that the appearance of the ruins in the Sacred Area is chaotic, and the damage so complete, that only wall-footings and silhouettes on the cliff remain. Keith and I used to sit on some fallen marble columns on the small plain of the sacrificial area in front of the cliff and puzzle our brains for a clue to the discovery, that we felt was right here, under our very eyes, if we could only spot it.

It is surprising, sometimes what small events change our whole outlook. One day when we were still contemplating the debris, the custodian happened to come along and say, "Those cyclopean blocks are thought to be the remains of a Samnite temple" . . . A temple! . . . This was the first temple we had seen, apart from those at Cuma. Immediately the aspect of the buildings on the Sacred Area, took on a new appearance. They were an architectural unit, the sanctuary attached to the temple. And the rooms and tunnels in Section III were indeed the monastery of the Cimmerians about which Ephorus had spoken.

We felt we were at last on the threshold of success. It was here that the Oracle was to be found.

At this same talk with the custodian, he told us there was a tunnel under the temple, which they had entered at the time of the excavation, but were unable to penetrate any distance, on account of foul air. The Inspector of Antiquities had given orders, that no one was to risk further exploration. So from then on, no one had attempted to enter. We decided to examine all these entries systematically, but we were somewhat scared by the talk of foul air in the tunnel under the temple. We decided to leave that until the last.

The first one we tackled, we named the Tomb Tunnel. This is situated on the level above the Sacred Area, some 20 feet above the datum that we had established at the bottom step of the service stair to the south of the temple. (Our datum is 75 feet above sea level.) The entry is from a large porch, about eight feet square with a gabled roof, if this can describe the triangular section of the roof of the porch. It was full of trusses of hay. We used these to make a camouflage, behind which we could work.

The first 20 feet of the tunnel was filled to the roof with loose earth. We made ourselves a pair of steel scoops, which we could slip over our hands. With these we scraped the earth away, burrowing like rabbits. We had not the slightest idea what we might find on the other side of the block. For all we knew it might be a well-shaft. So, when we had cleared a hole, that we could just squeeze through, lying flat, we first sampled the air, to make sure it was breathable, then one of us went through with a rope around his feet. Once over the blockage we found a good passage about four feet high by two feet wide. There was a lot of loose earth on the floor and we assumed that it was originally about six feet high.

The passage was almost straight on a bearing of 280 degrees. At the end of 48 feet, we found a massive rectangular doorway. The side posts and lintel were of hard dark grey lava, and the rabet for the door was on the outside. Passing through this, we found ourselves in a large vaulted room 21 feet long by 9 feet wide by 15 feet high. One half of the floor, longitudinally, was raised to form a bench 4 feet above the floor. Opposite the entrance door was a small door in the bench giving access to a tunnel. This tunnel traversed the whole length of the room and passed through the walls at either side. The dimensions of the tunnel were 18 inches wide by 30 inches high. Keith went in and I followed. We could see that the north end was blocked by thick deposits of hard stalagmite of unknown width, precluding any entry until it could be removed. We could, however crawl down the tunnel towards the south. The floor was deceptively smooth and we pushed on, carrying torches and our baskets with cameras, compass and measuring tape etc. We proceeded for 50 yards without any change in the shape or dimensions of the tunnel. Suddenly we realised, the dimensions would not permit us to turn round. Backing out, in that confined space for 50 knee scraping yards, very nearly cured us of tunnel exploration. But the results were up to our highest hopes. We knew now that we had really found the *argillae* of the Cimmerians, exactly as described by Ephorus.

Still on this upper level, we next explored the entry above

the silhouette, we later called the "Big 'D' Bath". Twenty feet
into the cliff face brought us to the top of some steps leading
down to the floor of a large cistern (the south tank). This platform is 7 feet above the floor, the total height of the tank being
15 feet to the top of the vaulted roof. The floor plan is a rectangle, 16 feet by 9 feet, with the bearing of the long axis 337
degrees. These dimensions are approximate, as the weight of
the overlying rock has resulted in a slight displacement, so that
the plan of the floor is not quite a true rectangle. Immediately
to the north of this, is another cistern with the same floor level
(13 feet above datum), separated from the south tank by a wall
3 feet thick.

At first glance, they appear to be twin structures. There are,
however, some very significant differences. The floor plan of
the north tank is truly rectangular, 19 feet by 13 feet and
approximately 15 feet to the vault of the roof. The long axis is
on a bearing of 330 degrees (the same as the line of the face of
the cliff and the silhouettes of the Sanctuary buildings). In the
vault of the roof are clear signs of conversion from a larger
space. At the level of the platform, in the east wall, there appear
to be blocked light shafts, and an access to a passage. There
are no stairs in this tank leading down to the floor level and
the only connection with the south tank, is by a hole at floor
level one foot high and nine inches wide, obviously a water
conduit. We could get into it by a large rough hole at platform
level, through the dividing wall. This hole was undoubtedly
made by a "grave robber", who entered the south tank at floor
level by a hole in the south east corner. He came through from
a passage (the debris he made in digging the hole all lies in the
passage). We went through his hole, and found ourselves in a
passage partly filled with rubble. The passage is three feet wide
with standing height. It extends towards the south-east in a
curve, until it lies directly over the axis of the main tunnel
leading west from the temple. Our survey shows that it finishes
behind the blockage in the Grotto in the temple. The actual
finish in the passage cannot be seen owing to an earth fall,
which came through a circular shaft. We checked the position
of this on the level above and found that it comes to the surface
in a small building, the wall footings of which, are visible beside
the service ramp leading to the higher terraces of the town.

There are traces of a door-stop in the curve of the passage, which may well have been a back way into the temple. Our survey also proved that the north wall of the north tank lies directly behind and in line with the north wall of the Painted Room on the level below. What is more, there is no resemblance between these tanks, and the Tomb Tunnel only 50 feet to the north.

Realisation of this, caused us to re-examine the immediate area. We saw that, what we had designated the Sacred Area, comprised a space about 100 feet long by 80 feet wide, on the piece of "solid ground" raised 6 feet above Section III, to which it was connected by a flight of steps. At the top of these steps are the ruins of an ancient arch. This is the northern limit of the Sacred Area, and the north wall of the Painted Room and north wall of the north tank lie on the line of the arch. The southern limit of the buildings, is the south wall of the temple, against which ascends the service ramp referred to previously. All this can be seen on the Plan 3. Looking from the front towards the cliff, the buildings clearly form two architectural sub-units. One on the right or north, comprises the Painted Room, the Big 'D', and the Sudatorium. The left hand unit comprises the temple and the original entrance. The division is solely on the shape of the silhouettes. Wall footings extend out from the cliff face, showing that the original buildings were vaulted-roof structures, similar to the rest in the terraces of the town. Other than this, the ruins are so damaged, that any further suggestions as to reconstruction are out of the question.

Nothing now to be seen on the surface, except the cyclopean blocks, is other than Roman. Nevertheless all the silhouettes bear evident traces of a concerted conversion, or camouflage from former usage. I shall describe these in detail as we come to them. We felt that the date of these conversions was a key point. We therefore asked M. W. Frederiksen, Fellow of Worcester College, Oxford, an authority on these matters to assist us. He visited the site and stated as his opinion, that much of the work was of Augustan age and that there was also a lot of Neronian work. In some cases the Neronian is superimposed on the Augustan, in what seems to be extensive repair work. I think we can date these repairs with some confidence, to damage following the great earthquake of A.D. 63 that caused so

much damage round the Bay of Naples. But more important
still, Mr. Frederiksen said, quite definitely the cyclopean walls
of the temple are not Samnite but Greek, probably of the sixth
or fifth century B.C. and that the little building had the appearance of the *cella* of a temple.

We now felt fairly certain that we had found something of
importance, but we were still a long way from knowing what.

By now we were making very careful measurements, both
dimensional and of compass bearings. We refer the levels to a
datum we established at the bottom of the last step of the service ramp. The height of the datum is 75 feet above sea level.
We put all our measurements on paper, in plan and in elevation.
The maze of passages and chambers behind the cliff face gradually became intelligible, as we continued our search.

One might ask why we did not, at once tackle the tunnel
under the temple, when all the time, this seemed the obvious
place to look, if indeed the Oracle was to be found in the ruins.
It is always easy to be wise after the event. As our hopes and
feelings in this great discovery, are an atmosphere that I want
readers to share, let us sit for a moment, as Keith and I did for
long periods, and look at the ruins and the cliff face again from
the front (the east). At this time we had no idea what form the
Oracle might have. The Grotto in the temple, has approximately, the same section, height and width, as the Antrum of
the Sibyl at Cuma. I think that, at the back of our minds, we
rather expected the Oracle of the Dead to be something similar.
The blockage in the Grotto and the passage behind leading to
the south tank, all tended to confuse the issue in our minds.
Further, in spite of the fact that Mr. Frederiksen was positive
about the 'temple', it seemed a poor little building for such a
great purpose. We did not realise at that time that the *cella* of
the temple is the holy of holies, the residence of the god, thus
forming only a part of the temple proper.[16]

The chief custodian told us that when the excavations were
carried out, the debris of these five buildings was no different
from that of any others in the general remains of the terrace
vaults.

There are a number of broken columns of white marble,
lying on the space in front (the Sacrificial Area), which, at first,
we thought, had perhaps adorned the façade of the temple.

There are no signs of column bases or any extension of the temple beyond 'the building line', delineated by a long wall footing, connecting the outer wall of the temple with the outer wall of the Painted Room. Discussing these columns with the chief custodian, he expressed the opinion that they had fallen down from a higher terrace, possibly that on which the Dioscuri were found, some 30-40 feet above.

In the wall of the building line, there are numerous repairs of Roman date. Some of these are blockages to entries leading from the Sacrificial Area into the various rectangles of which the silhouettes on the cliff face form the western end. With this meagre evidence, only a hypothetical reconstruction can be attempted. It seems likely that there were five vaulted chambers, the temple, the original entrance, the Sudatorium, the Big 'D', and the Painted Room. There was a narrow vaulted passage separating the Big 'D' from the Sudatorium.

How far the level above extended over these vaults, as a flat or with structures upon it, is indeterminable.

There are no remains of any of the eastern or of the southern limits. The eastern walls were doubtless destroyed when Section IV was built in A.D. 80. Excavations are still in progress to the south and some discoveries may yet be made there.

The eastern aspect of the five buildings must have been very severe. Maybe this was intentional in view of the dread rites of darkness and death that were celebrated.

We are reasonably certain that we explored every hollow space behind the cliff face and we are sure there is no large room behind the Painted Room, although there is ample space for one, between the back wall and the north tank. The remains of the Roman arch at the top of the steps leading to Section III appears to indicate that here was one of the principal entrances, giving onto the Forecourt with the two 'D' baths, and the marble table feet.

The Big 'D' has communication with the Painted Room, but is isolated from the other buildings by the passage leading to the stair behind the present statue niche. Nevertheless the Painted Room and the Big 'D', undoubtedly form part of the original complex; as they not only have the same orientation, but the north wall of the Painted Room and that of the north tank lie on the same line. One might hazard a guess that these were the chambers of the Sanctuary, to which the public had access.

The Sudatorium next compelled our attention. With the exception of the very similar chamber in the complex of the *argillae* under the chapel of Sosandra, in Section III, there are no buildings like it at Baiae. We knew of the account given by Pausanias of his descent to the Oracle of Trophonius at Labadeia in Greece.[13] Was the Sudatorium a similar *Tholos* entrance. These round bottle-shaped buildings with the entrance at the top and an outlet at the bottom facing east, had a long history. They can still be seen today in East Africa, where they are grass huts used as ghost houses, containing raised platforms upon which the corpses are laid. When the migrants from this area crossed the Straits of Bab-el-Mandeb to Arabia and worked their way up the coast of the Red Sea to Palestine and Asia Minor, they brought these ghost houses with them and they were adopted as their tombs by the Myceneans.

We are of opinion that the Sudatorium and the other chamber under Sosandra, are ghost houses of this type, forming a suitable entry to this place of mystery and death. This deduction stimulated us the more, as the passage under the floor leads back to the main tunnel.

The Sudatorium was in existence, before the passages to the south tank from the Grotto were cut, as is obvious from their alignment. This in turn suggests that the Grotto is of later date than the main tunnel. All this seems simple now, but at this time their significance was problematical.

All the surface masonry is Roman and at first glance there is nothing to suggest conversion from former usage. The ruins present much the same general appearance as any others at Baiae. The various buildings on the Sacred Area appear to be . . . just what they pretend to be . . . thermal baths.

It was the stucco screen that had been placed over the vault of the original entrance, that led to our intuition, that we were looking at camouflage. From the front, one sees a lower vaulted silhouette, forming a slight alcove into the cliff face, perhaps eighteen inches deep, the face being formed by *opus reticulatum* (diamond-shaped block masonry of Augustan date). Into this face were driven numerous iron sprags, upon which was built the stucco screen, the sprags serving as keys to hold it to the masonry. A small section of the fluted stucco remains in the corner of the vaulted roof, at the upper left hand. We found later, that there is a room behind this, and a passage connecting with the main tunnel. We think, that formerly the stuccoed recess took in this room and formed an ante-room to the passage, especially, as above the recess is another corresponding silhouette, some six feet higher up, presumably forming the original roof of the building.

The dating of all this work by Mr. Frederiksen as Augustan, and references to the suppression of the Shrines of Apollo round Lake Avernus, triggered the intuition, that here we were looking at the same efforts at camouflage.[14]

This realisation, enabled us tentatively, to ascribe the temple to Apollo. This was a chain reaction which led us to recall that Apollo had the habit of appropriating ancient Oracles belonging to the Great Goddess. He had the temple at Cuma which was so closely connected with the Sibyl, and the Sibyl was connected in some way with the Oracle of the Dead, as she plays such a large part in Vergil's story.

At this stage, we should also note, that the custodians had told us, that it was the official opinion, that the tunnel leading from the trench under the temple, was a water conduit pure and simple. At first glance there is nothing incompatible with that view. The sides of the trench are thickly coated with calcareous deposit, so is the floor of the tunnel for several feet from the entrance. Also, that when they had attempted to enter, they found the way dangerous on account of foul air. It was only by careful survey and levelling, that we found the fall of ten feet, to be inwards towards the hill, thus disposing of the water conduit theory. But of course we did not know this at the time we are now considering. As a matter of fact we had not the slightest idea that we were actually looking at the entrance of the Great Antrum, later found to extend for nearly three hundred yards into the hill.

We descended into the trench and saw the pipe, lying on a shelf. This was the pipe leading to the rear of the Sudatorium, and then the artificial roof forming the floor of the Grotto. Careful drawing of the passages in plan and elevation, proved to us that a considerable amount of building construction, had also been carried out in the main tunnel entrance in Augustan times. Reference to Fig. 3 will reveal that there is a second cliff face (it is in fact the cliff face on the terrace, 20 feet above datum). It can also be seen to the south of the temple. Examination of the south wall of the temple shows a vertical division where the *opus reticulatum* of the temple wall adjoins a rough masonry filler-wall. This wall forms the end wall of the Room of Memory. One gets the impression that the space we are calling the Room of Memory, was originally a passage behind and between the temple and the face of the cliff, which had been roofed over at some later date.

Descending again into the trench, several features can be distinguished. The eastern extension of the trench is one yard wide and orientated on a bearing of 275 degrees. At a point 6 feet from the north-west corner of the temple, the trench narrows to a width of 21 inches, and at the same time the bearing changes to 270 degrees. Thus the centre line of the trench passes under the north-west corner. Doubtless the reason for this, is the well known precept of ancient divination, that the north-west quadrant was sacred to the Fates and the gods of the Nether Regions.

Continuing west along the trench, it is seen that while the south wall is solid rock, the north wall is block masonry for a distance of 24 feet, 6 inches, to where the original entrance joins. The original entrance is not at right angles to the cliff face, but orientated on 250 degrees and both walls of the adit are lined with tufa masonry. Also in the main tunnel, is a branch leading to the south about twenty feet long situated 5 feet east of the original entrance junction.

We have spent much time in endeavouring to account for these features but without result. Maybe the original floor level was at the trench bottom, and this was an ante-room to the main tunnel. The main tunnel apparently began here, as the edges of the walls, where they meet the original entrance are arrissed. The orientation of the 'original' entrance also shows that it was a later addition, probably following earthquake damage.

Reconstruction of the interior of the temple to its original is quite impossible. Apart from the big blocks all the masonry is Roman, and apparently of several dates. Quite a lot of it is even Neronian brickwork.

The blockage in the Grotto above appears to have been connected with a vent whereby the lamp smoke was removed from the underground tunnels. Later, we found over 500 lamp niches in the complex of the Oracle.

Our base for the measurements of the underground tunnels is the point where the trench narrows in the temple. We are confident that from here onwards, all is original work.

In the main tunnel, which owing to its bearing we named '270', just opposite the end of the passage leading to the Sudatorium, there is a large square tile in the roof. If the axis of the passage in the room behind the west wall of the temple (the Room of Memory) be extended, it would intersect the 270 at this point. We should like to remove the tile to prove this.

The question of exploring the tunnel under the temple was now our constant topic of conversation, as by now we were convinced that the end of our search was here. We were still scared by the stories of foul gas. In order to check the various passages that I have already mentioned we had already been in, as far as the back of the Sudatorium—that is some 50 feet— and the air was perfectly good. We were also aware that it is not normally possible to ventilate a tunnel of any length, that has only one entrance. Coal mines have two shafts, one to carry the fresh air in and the other to take the foul air out. Unless this tunnel went right through the hill, to come out at Fusaro, we felt sure there would be foul air in it. The first task was to inspect the Fusaro side of the hill. This we did, asking all the farmers if they had any holes in their fields. We also asked all the small boys, as we thought they would know, if anyone did. We satisfied ourselves there was no possibility of a through passage. So we were back with our problem. Eventually we decided we would make the attempt. We roped a volunteer member of our team on the end of a 25-foot rope. The idea was that he marched forward to the limit of the rope. If he stood up we assumed the air to be good . . . if he fell down we hoped we should be able to pull him back to safety. It worked without anybody falling down.

In the dust on the floor we could see the footprints of the excavators who had entered the tunnel in 1958. These ceased . . . and we saw in front of us, the clean virgin dust of the floor stretching away into the darkness of the tunnel. . . . We were

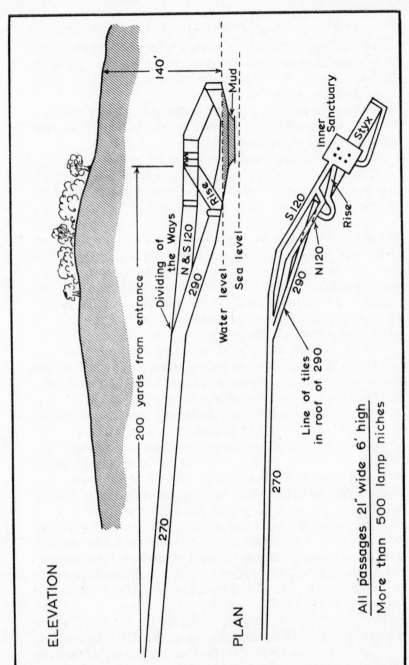

ELEVATION

140'

200 yards from entrance

Dividing of
the Ways

N & S 120

290

Rise

Mud

Water level

Sea level

270

PLAN

Line of tiles
in roof of 290

270

290

S 120

N 120

Rise

Inner
Sanctuary

Styx

All passages 21" wide 6' high
More than 500 lamp niches

Fig. 4. The Oracle of the Dead

the first people in there for 2,000 years. The atmosphere was full of dust which got worse as we went forward. The temperature began to rise rapidly, until we were all perspiring freely and thoroughly frightened. We went in for 400 feet, until we reached a point where the tunnel started to go downwards. We decided we had had enough for one day, and beat a rapid retreat back to daylight and fresh air.

We agreed to designate the various tunnels by their compass bearings as a means of identification. We called this 400-foot-long entrance tunnel '270' which is True West on the 360-degree compass.

Owing to the Italian qualms about the foul air, we decided to keep our explorations secret until we could decide what we had found.

We soon got our courage back and went in again. This time we reached the 400 foot point, which later we called 'The Dividing of the Ways'. We then continued down the long slope, 150 feet until we were stopped by water (see Fig. 4). Here we found the temperature was 120° F. and at the same time there was shortage of oxygen that made breathing very difficult. There was a tunnel entry off to the right but it was filled completely with loose earth. The air was so bad that we could only stay down at the water for about fifteen minutes at the outside. The dust laden atmosphere made it very difficult to see anything in the small illumination from electric hand torches. So we took photographs by flash on colour film, at every stage, so that we could enlarge them on a screen and study them under better conditions. One of these photographs showed a large tile in the roof above the water. We thought that this might be a cover to some opening, so we gave it a push and were able to move it to one side. It left a hole 18 inches square, and naturally Keith had to climb through. He found himself at the bottom of a steeply sloping tunnel, at the top of which was, apparently, a door blocked with tufa masonry. The air was even hotter than at the water and in five minutes he was back. We sat at the water's edge and discussed this new situation. Looking around us at the walls of the tunnel, we noticed that one of the niches had a stain running down from it. Keith said, "That looks uncommonly like an oil stain", and then I realised we were looking at a lamp niche. Examination of others confirmed this. In

H

some cases the imprint of the shape of the bottom of the lamp could be clearly seen. We counted the niches and found that in the total there were more than 500.

At this moment I realised we had found the Oracle of the Dead.

These 500 lamps, could only indicate the use of the tunnel for some great ceremonial and the blocked up door at the top of the Rise that Keith had seen through the tile-hole was "The Sanctuary of the Cimmerians far beneath the Earth", that Ephorus had described.

People have asked us, What did you do? Go and have a drink on it, or tell the world.

We did neither. I think we were completely awed by our good fortune. We were sitting at the edge of the water at the time. We had not yet found the return passages and had only had a glimpse at the Inner Sanctuary. But we just knew we were sitting on the banks of the River Styx. We both drank some of the water, and found it as Ephorus had said. "There is a fount of potable water, but people refrain from its use, because they say it is the water of the River Styx."

This was September 21st, 1962. Another year was to pass before we had explored the full 880 feet of passages in this wonderful place. Keith managed to scramble his way over three 20-foot long earth blocks in the return passages and to measure them and get compass bearings in an incredible atmosphere of heat and dust. Another thrill was, when after waiting for more than an hour at the 400 foot point, I heard Keith tapping behind a concrete wall, which he had reached after crawling through 350 feet of unknown tunnel on a hunch that they would finish at this point.

We now knew the full extent of the complex. We also knew that there were certain points where there were special landmarks. I do not remember when we first began to associate Vergil with the tunnels. Keith read the *Aeneid* again, because he had originally felt the road down to the House of Persephone and the Elysian Fields must have gone right through the hill, as Vergil speaks of the Sun and the Stars shining on the Fields of Joy. Then outside the door of the Inner Sanctuary, we found a large niche about a foot above the floor. It did not seem that a position so close to the floor was consistent with the idea of a niche for a torch. Was it the niche, in which to place the Golden Bough, the mistletoe which was the pilgrim's passport for his return to the upper world. There are many other coincidences with the Vergil story, about which I shall speak later.[15]

We also solved the ventilation problem. Somewhere down at the water level, there is a hot gas vent, puffing out carbonic acid. This heats the air up to 120° F. Hot air rises and does in fact rise up the steep slope to the Inner Sanctuary and out along the roof of the return passages while a current of cold air flows in along the floor. The smoke and foul air all enhanced the illusion of the Entrance to Hell. Before the passages were blocked up by Agrippa, the ventilation system was doubtless excellent. Today, all the foul air has to pass up the one passage which makes the process slower and accounts for the foul air, and bad conditions now existing.

Another thing that amazed us, was the perfect state of preservation of the tunnels, not a crack anywhere in the walls and not a change of level or displacement due to earthquake. In spite of the total destruction presumably by earthquake, of the surface buildings before they were buried, it would seem as if underground structures are immune from shock damage. Maybe this was one of the things that enhanced the sanctity of the Oracle in the eyes of the ancients.

The hillside at Baiae is still in sympathetic contact with the general volcanic forces in the Phlegrean Fields. When Solfatara is very active, the hot springs and gas orifices all round the region act in unison. Even within the ruins themselves conditions are very variable. Although the Styx water has remained cool and fresh as long as we have known it, other springs in the ruins are very different. There is a spring behind the Piscina of Mercury which, one week flows with a discharge of hundreds of gallons an hour of boiling water. The very next week there will be a trickle of cold water, forming stagnant pools in which mosquitoes breed by the thousand.

Once the discovery was made, the proofs soon amounted to reasonable certainty. The whole idea of an Oracle of the Dead near Avernus, had gradually, over the centuries, become confused and finally was deemed a poetic invention. We had to dispel this illusion, and also to place on permanent record, the details of our discovery.

We have tried to establish the history of the Oracle. There is very little direct evidence. I think we can accept the *Odyssey* as proving that it was functioning in 1000 B.C. By that time its fame had spread over all the known world, reaching Asia Minor where Homer lived and wrote. This indicates a long period of activity prior to this. The Pelasgians were the first to establish Oracles in the mainland of Greece, the oldest being at Dordona in Epirus. This Oracle had direct contact with the Lybian Oracle at Ammon in North Africa. The first people at Cuma were probably a colony from Gaudo, which had been settled by a Lybian people prior to 2500 B.C. Who knows if the Oracle was not founded by these Stone Age men.[16]

The Oracle was buried by a landslide, probably as the result of a great earthquake in the reign of Nero, A.D. 63 when many of the towns round the Bay of Naples including Pompeii and Herculaneum were practically destroyed. These towns were scarcely built up again when they were finally buried by Vesuvius in A.D. 79.

Pliny the Elder writing in about A.D. 75, in his description of the coast round here says, "there was formerly a city of the Cimmerians". He gives no other information. One wonders why? We think it possible that another earthquake had occurred during the period when the conversions were being made by Agrippa. This might have resulted in the blocking of the underground parts of the Oracle and these were never reopened. The surface buildings continued to function as a community centre for many more years. This explanation which is in some degree supported by evidence, may account for Pliny's silence on the subject.[17]

If the Sanctuary still continued to operate it must have been very different from the pageantry of the Cimmerians. Section III had been built and most of the *argillae* destroyed in the process. The religious rites were in keeping with the times: Orphic initiations, meetings of the new Christian believers. Minerva seems to have become the dominant divinity at Baiae. Nero came every year to celebrate her festival on March 19th and the following five days.

Speculation on these things is a great temptation. Keith and I are anxious to avoid misunderstandings. I shall give a technical account of our discoveries in the next chapter, so that any archaeologist who wishes can check our plans and put his own interpretation on them can do so. But the spice of archaeology is in re-creating the past, so, after the technical description, Chapter V will endeavour to revive the ancient rites at the Oracle, by comparison with the description of similar Oracles given by Greek historians and poets.

When visiting the site of the Oracle today, the first reaction may be one of disappointment. The utter ruin of the surface buildings has deprived the visitor of the preliminaries to actual descent to the Oracle. Then again the modern cynical sceptic finds it difficult to school his thoughts so that he can imagine himself a pilgrim about to visit the most sacred spot on the whole earth . . . the Entrance to Paradise.

Remember this when you visit Baiae.

NOTES

1. Herodotus, II, 53.
2. The Bible, The Book of Jonah.
3. Homer, *Odyssey*, X.
4. Homer, *op. cit.*, XI.
5. Strabo, v, 4, 5.
6. *ibid.*
7. *ibid.*
8. Amadeo Maiuri, *The Phlegrean Fields.*
9. *ibid.*
10. September, 1538.
11. All bearings are *true* geographical.
12. Pliny the Younger, *Letters to his Friends*, VI, 16.
13. Pausanias, VIII, 28-31.
14. Strabo, v, 4, 5.
15. Vergil, *Aenid*, VI.
16. P. G. Sestieri, *Guide to Paestum.*
17. Pliny the Elder, *Historia Naturalis.*

4

Identifying the Oracle

We now knew that we had found the Oracle of the Dead, about which Ephorus had written five hundred years before the birth of Christ. But we were still faced with the problem of marshalling the proofs, so that the archaeological world would also accept our beliefs. The whole site was mysterious. Except for a few jagged walls, until 1956 there had been no indication that buried here under the vineyards was a complete town. The cover of volcanic ash and dust was more than twenty feet thick. Throughout the Middle Ages there had been only rough forest and small cultivated plots. The modern town of Baia originated in quite recent times, as a ribbon development along the sea front when the road from Pozzuoli to Bacoli was completed at the beginning of the century. I have a book written twenty years ago by Professor Schiano, and he obviously, had no idea of the extent of the ruins at Baiae. It was assumed that Roman Baiae had disappeared under the waters of the bay, due to bradyseism, or had been destroyed in the eruption of Monte Nuovo. Any idea of an Oracle of the Dead was dismissed as a legend, created by the *Odyssey* and the *Aeneid*. The references by Ephorus were not taken seriously. The three domed buildings, more or less at beach level, were supposed by the archaeologists of the early 1900s to be temples and were named, Temples of Diana, Mercury, and Venus. It is now known that they are swimming pools, yet for some extraordinary reason the Italian authorities still label them as temples.

Since the excavations were carried out in 1956-58, no scientific research work has been done at Baiae, with the exception of an architectural commission which endeavoured to recapture the original design.

We were, unquestionably, the first to apply method to the problem. The architectural commission failed, because they started from the mistaken premise, that the ruins were those of thermae (baths). They suggested that the water had been brought to the site by an aqueduct at the top of the ridge and then allowed to fall by gravity down through the various terraces, servicing baths and fountains in the process, finally to be collected in the big 'temples' at sea level. The hot gas and hot water were supposed to come from many orifices at various levels on the terraces. There is no evidence today of there having been any gas or water orifices on the terrace with two exceptions: one in Section II behind the Piscina of Mercury and the other in Section IV about halfway down the terraces, at the level of the theatre. All the evidence points to these being the only sources of hot water and gas in the upper part of the ruins. From these points the requirements were pumped and piped to the various Sudatoria. There are still hot water springs at sea level, at the junction between the crater wall and the floor. This phenomenon applies to all the craters in the Phlegrean Fields. Where there are still hot springs they are all along the junction of the wall and floor which is a line of weakness in the crust.

Roman Baiae is not in the Bay, but lies along the dyke that separates Lake Lucrino from the sea. On the floor of the Bay of Baiae there are only a few large buildings, a line of marble columns along the three fathom line, which was the former sea front, along which the road passed between the two points of the bay. The probable reason why there are no houses or other extension of the thermae on the floor of the bay is bradyseism. Even in Roman times, Horace and Strabo both mention the necessity for constantly raising the road to keep it above sea level.

In order that the evidence may not be confused by speculation, I propose in this chapter, to give a detailed technical description of the complex of galleries behind the temple. Our conclusions will be dealt with in the next chapter.

The terrace town is an anomaly, unless the existence of the Oracle with its need for servicing is admitted.

We found consistent evidence, both on the surface and underground, of conversion and camouflage, disguising the buildings and tunnels. It is known that at the time of the war between

Octavian and first Pompey then Antony, the Roman Admiral
Agrippa suppressed the cult of Apollo, within the crater of
Avernus, razing all the shrines to the ground, and replacing
them with slipways and dockyards. This was the occasion when
this sacrilege so infuriated the god that his statue in his temple
in Rome broke into perspiration, and a great storm blew continuously in the Bay of Naples. Only after the Pontifex Maximus had sacrificed hecatombs of victims was Apollo appeased
and the storm subsided. This frightened Agrippa, and instead
of destroying the Sanctuary and Oracle at Baiae, he resorted
to conversion and camouflage. Details of his efforts will be
given in the appropriate place. The dating of the operation was
made by Mr. M. W. Frederiksen, as I have already indicated.

Remembering that the Romans were here from 334 B.C., it is
not at all surprising that none but Roman masonry is to be seen.
Only the ground plan remains of the former buildings. We also
think that the architectural commission did not realise that the
apparently innumerable reconstructions were in the main major
repairs following severe earthquake damage, but that the general design and layout was not altered. So in the temple, the
Romans left the Greek blocks in place where they could, and
reconstructed round them. I think we still see the original Greek
supporting walls for the wooden floor. But all the rest of it is of
Augustan or even Neronian date.

The trench is 7 feet 6 inches deep, below our datum level. It
traverses the temple diagonally on a bearing of 275 degrees.
In the temple, on this bearing it is 3 feet wide, lined with
brick vertical columns 2 feet apart. The sides of the trench
are thickly covered with a crystalline calcareous deposit, down
to within 3 feet of the floor. It is obvious that here the floor
was covered with rubbish to this depth and this was removed
by the excavators in 1956. This deposit is confined to the part
of the trench in the temple, and it shows that there must have
been an open space, filled with water for a very long period.
This water was rain water, which dissolved the salts out of the
tufa and redeposited them on the sides of the trench during dry
spells. Three feet above the floor, on the south side of the
trench, there is a shelf running the full length, upon which at
intervals are the remains of terracotta pipe. The diameter of the
pipe is the same as that of the hole in the blockage at the end

of the passage leading to the Sudatorium. Here we have the solution of the method of heating. The hot gas was led from the orifice lower down the hillside, by means of this terracotta pipe. This discovery disposed of one of the arguments that the excavators used to prove that this long tunnel was merely a hot water conduit.

The trench passes directly under the north-western angle of the temple wall. Six feet to the east of this point the trench narrows to 21 inches wide, and changes its bearing to 270 degrees. It retains these measurements for 400 feet. Standing in the bottom of the trench at this point and looking up, a series of brick arches are seen, which support the floor of the Grotto, which lies above and parallel to the axis of the trench.

The Grotto opens out from the temple into the cliff. The floor is 6 feet 6 inches above datum, and the height is about nine feet, the width is 4 feet; 15 feet from the entrance is the blockage. This is very interesting; the lower left half of the blockage is a solid stucco-covered block, whilst the lower right half and all the upper part is rough walling. In the centre of the top half is a square manhole formed by tiles. This enabled the rear of the blockage to be filled right up to the roof. The same technique will be seen later with the blockage at the Inner Sanctuary at the far end of the tunnel complex, thus suggesting that the work was done by the same team of men.

I have mentioned that the lower right half of the blockage, at the side of the stucco section is rough walling. It gives the impression of having been a passage to the rear of the blockage. Our survey proved that this passage eventually leads to the south tank, situated above and behind the Big 'D'. The names I use in the text will identify these items on the plans.

Comparing the position of the blockage, with indications down in the trench, one can see that this was a 'smokeface', to draw the smoke up towards the chimney, where the foul air from the galleries was evacuated. Traces of this chimney can be seen in the passage behind the blockage. On the right (north at a distance of 5 feet 3 inches from the line of the smoke face is the junction of the trench with the original entrance. This point was apparently, the true beginning of the tunnel. Between here and the cliff face, there is a lot of tufa masonry in blocks about the size of a modern brick. Here we are at least 17 feet inside the cliff, and the only explanation is that formerly there was some kind of chamber here as an ante-room to the tunnel. The edges of the tunnel junction walls are all arrissed. We designated the tunnel '270' after its bearing.

It is fortunate that the excavators cleared the debris from the trench right down to the floor, as this gave us the dimensions of the tunnel. Originally it was 8 feet high by 21 inches wide. Owing to the passage of time, there is a deposit of crystalline material on the floor, about three feet thick. There is also a thin deposit on the walls.

For the first twenty feet or so, there is some rubble on the floor, but soon the floor becomes quite smooth. Today's dimensions are about six feet high by twenty-one inches wide. At no place throughout the whole complex, is there any sign of earthquake damage, or change of level due to 'weight', or cracks or damage due to bradyseism.

The vault of the roof is semi-circular, the walls are clean and smooth, but not lined in any way. On both sides, at intervals of 12 feet, alternately, is a lamp niche. Owing to the fill on the floor, these are now at a height of about three feet six inches. In the old days they were just about head level. Fifty-five feet from the entrance on the right is the circular hole in the wall, blocking the passage leading to the Sudatorium. This passage has been reduced in height by half, during the conversion by the Romans. Originally it was an imposing tunnel 8 feet high and 21 inches wide. The round 'tholos'-shaped Sudatorium is also unique in the ruins; the other 'sweatrooms' are all rectangular. The presence of the imposing passage way, allows the justifiable deduction that this was indeed, a tholos-type of building, similar to that at the Oracle of Trophonius at Lebadeia in Greece.

In the roof of the 270 passage at the junction with the Sudatorium tunnel, there is a large tile in the roof, some 18 inches square, which we have not disturbed. It lies at a point on the axis of a passage, leading from the room behind the west wall of the temple, which is now blocked. We consider this to be part of the Roman conversion.

Continuing on towards the west, at 150 feet there is a widening of the passage for about six feet in length to a width of about two feet six inches. There is not enough room for two people to pass, so we concluded, that this enlargement was due, perhaps to accidental composition of the tufa, necessitating cutting back to get a clean surface. The tufa contains several strata of rough texture with quite large boulders. It may well have been something of this kind.

Tunnel 270 continues due west, in a perfectly straight line, for 408 feet. At the same time there is a slight fall, amounting in all to 10 feet. This is further proof that the tunnel is not a water conduit, or the fall would not be into the hill. We found later that the fall is part of the ventilation system.

Just before reaching the end of the 270, the strict rectilinear axis of the tunnel is maintained, whilst the walls make a shallow S-bend, in such a manner that what lies at the end of the tunnel may not be seen until the last moment. This same technique is followed at other key points. It seems to have been deliberate, to produce a dramatic arrival at these points.

At the end of 270, there is a change of direction of the tunnel. At this point, there is a small wedge-shaped chamber, narrowing towards the west end. Closer examination tells the story. This chamber, which we call Dividing of the Ways is created by the sudden widening of 270, on the right by 12 inches and on the left by 4 inches. Standing within the 270 and looking west, it is seen that the left side is a wall, blocking the tunnel diagonally (see Fig. 5). If that wall were not there, 270 would continue westwards on the same level to intersect with the return passages. At the west end of the wall, in the floor, is a door cardinal. The whole chamber is seen to be designed for the operation of this door. Its purpose was to shut off the continuation of 270, or the right fork of the tunnel at will.

I shall show that behind the wall there are galleries, which we designated North 120 and South 120. We proved this and the thickness of the wall by Keith hammering on the far side whilst I traced the position of the blows with my hand on the 270 side of the wall. It is only a few inches thick.

The fork to the right, is a ramp and step stair with a bearing of 290 degrees. It is 150 feet long and descends 40 feet in that distance. The builders of Baiae were very fond of these ramp and step stairs. For the first 17 feet, the left hand side of the roof is composed of heavy red tiles. Until we proved the existence of the 120 passages, we were under the impression that

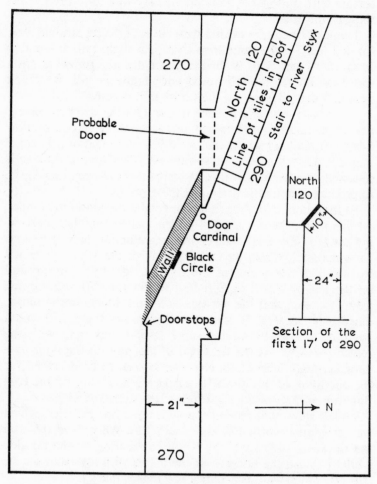

Fig. 5. THE DIVIDING OF THE WAYS

there was a room behind these walls. But again, by Keith tapping with a hammer and my location of the blows, enabled us to prove that the tiles cover the floor of the end of the North 120 passage. In other words before the Romans blocked it up, here was an open-ended passage. The door cardinal shows that one of the functions of the door was to control the smoke pouring into 290, from the inner galleries.

The Dividing of the Ways was evidently an important point in the tunnel complex.

The dimensions of the 290 stair are slightly larger than those of 270. The height was probably only about six feet (there is some fill on the floor but not enough to hide the steps), but the width is 26 inches and the lamp niches are only a yard apart and opposite each other. There are more than one hundred in all. The slope is not constant, as the upper 30 feet are almost one in two, the remainder being one in four, and the last 25 feet at the bottom are level.

There is a similar shallow S-bend, as we saw in 270, at the bottom end to hide the view.

The temperature at the bottom end rises suddenly to 120° F., and at the same time, the lack of oxygen in the atmosphere becomes very marked. Breathing becomes difficult, and on some occasions we were able to stay down for only a few minutes. At the time of our discovery, we were unable to account for this. Later in May 1965, Col. David Lewis, U.S. Army, dived into the Styx and made his spectacular discovery of the hot springs nearly thirty feet under water. The story of this exploit is given later.

This was also the secret of the ventilation of the tunnels. The hot point is the lowest point reached by the galleries. The hot air rises to the roof and flows out to daylight, whilst, at the same time, the circuit is completed, by a current of cold air running in along the floor. The system works today, in spite of the blockage of the 120 passages at the Dividing of the Ways, somewhat slowly but giving breathable air. It must have been very efficient, when the system of doors was controlling it, in the old days.

Beyond the S-bend in 290 is a level stretch for 25 feet. This ends at a series of steps forming a landing stage, to a considerable stretch of water. The landing stage widens 2 feet on the

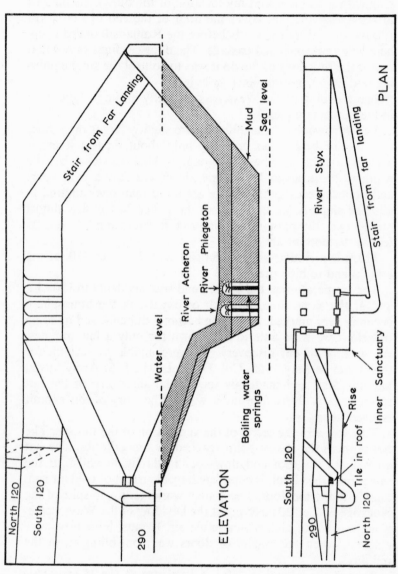

Fig. 6. The River Styx

left, and (6 feet further on), 2 feet on the right, making the water at least 6 feet wide at the commencement. The height from the roof to the water is approximately five feet and waterlines on the side walls show that the level has varied considerably in the past. In the three years that we have known it, it remained absolutely constant until May 1965. It then suddenly dropped nearly 2 feet in level, and has remained static. We assume that the cause is telluric, and connected with the general recrudescence of volcanic activity in the region, due to the predicted imminent resumption of activity by Vesuvius. Other hot springs in the ruins have been affected.

Five feet east of (that is, before reaching) the water there is an opening on the right in the 290. This is the entrance to the Rise. At this point the roof of the tunnel is 6 feet above the floor. Here the roof begins to get lower and meets the water at a distance of 15 feet from the Landing. At the same time the side walls of the water also close in until, at the point where the roof meets the water, the width of the tunnel is only 3 feet.

For a long time we had no idea of the possible further extension of the water, and we had always assumed that the apparent narrowing of the tunnel was the effect of perspective. We had no knowledge of the depth of the water, or how it was fed and discharged to keep fresh and at constant level. We could only infer from what we could see.

Finally, in May 1965, a good friend of ours Col. David Lewis, U.S. Army, and his son Warren Lewis undertook the exploration of the water by diving with air bottles. He found that the tunnel narrows vertically and horizontally for a distance of 24 feet. Apart from the descent of the roof the floor appears to rise also. This is due to the tendency of the floor deposits to find the level. This deposit consists of fine calcareous crystals, covering a rubble 'fill'. The depth of water at the landing is 2 feet and by the time the roof reaches the water it has increased to 6 feet. This shows that the floor actually slopes down at a considerable but unknown angle.

At 24 feet the roof suddenly takes a sharp steep slope downwards, and the floor corresponds. The drop amounts to 5 feet, when the roof levels out again. It remains level for at least 30 feet. The floor in the meanwhile, follows the roof contour and also drops 5 feet. The horizontal distance covered by the drop is 7 feet. The floor is now level and is still composed of the fine crystals of calcareous material. The surface of the mud, only 8 inches below the roof, along the south wall of the tunnel, which has now opened out to a width of about 6 feet, is covered with holes about one inch in diameter surrounded with pale mud. These holes are hot springs emitting very hot water in excess of 120° F. which was the maximum of our thermometer. It should be noted that the general temperature of the water at the landing is 85° F. Three feet from the bottom of the slope in the left or south wall, is a tunnel opening. Only about a foot of the arch is visible above the mud. Examination showed it to turn towards the east, and very hot water is issuing from it. It seems that this was the means whereby water was brought from a spring to the Styx tunnel. We named this side tunnel The River Acheron (see Fig. 6). About two feet west of this tunnel, is another, which could not be examined owing to the clouds of fine mud disturbed by the swimmers. We named it the River Phlegeton. But Col. Lewis continued to dive westwards for a further 20 feet, when the water was so hot he had to retreat. But he had seen that at this point the tunnel took a sharp bend to the right and began to rise steeply.

As Col. Lewis himself put it, he was so excited the first time he dived the Styx that he did not take due precautions not to disturb the mud. In consequence he decided to try again. So on November 26th, 1965 he made another attempt. This time with great success as can be seen from the marvellous photograph of the boiling source of the River Styx which he kindly gave me to illustrate this book. At the same time he went on past the hot springs and was able to see that the passage does in fact end in a stair, which coincided on our plans with the passage leading up to the north door of the Inner Sanctuary.

For good measure another friend Robert E. Love, Jr., also dived the Styx on February 13th, 1966. In spite of the inauspicious date Bob was able to penetrate into the chamber containing the hot springs. He found the two openings led into the same rough-hewn underwater cavern from which boiling water was issuing. But we are still unable to find where all this water goes to, in order that the constant level may be maintained.

It was a very eerie and awe-inspiring time sitting at the landing at the bottom of 290 waiting for the diver to return. He

The source of the River Styx. This picture is unique, and may never be repeated. It was taken by Colonel David Lewis some fifty feet below the surface of the Styx. The scene is one of the boiling water springs which are the river's sources. The dramatic clouds are the fine silt which was stirred up by the diver. The whole height of the clear water above the mud is only about eight inches and the diver's air bubbles were constantly scraping along the roof. The passage at this point is only three feet wide.

"The Writing on the Wall"—what do these mysterious letters mean? They are a foot high painted in red paint on the rough wall of The Traverse. Maybe they contain the clue to the name of the deity to whom the Great Antrum was dedicated. (See also Fig. 8 on page 134).

was underwater for more than half an hour. His progress could be followed by the glare and reflection in the water of his powerful torch. Every few seconds there was the weird gurgle of his air bubbles rising to the surface. As he took pictures the flash illuminated the whole of the River Styx with golden light. On three occasions the flash-lamp bulbs burst with a very frightening bang. What an experience. The ancient writers say that the only thing that can resist the corrosive action of the water of the River Styx is a horse's hoof. All I can say is that neoprene diving suits are equally immune, and Dave, Warren and Bob have something to remember for the rest of their lives, an utterly unique experience, that is not likely to be repeated by anyone.

The difficulties of exploration in water at a temperature around 100° F. are obvious and it is most unlikely that we shall be able to obtain any further information about these passages. It is a great tribute to the courage of these two men, that they dared to make this spectacular entry into an almost vertical shaft filled with 12 feet of hot water.

The water is quite clear and limpid and quite good to drink. The level is 15 feet above sea level. There are still many mysteries to be solved, that indeed may never be solved. We are satisfied that the latest discoveries made by diving, have not altered the general assumption, that this is the River Styx as conceived by the constructors of the Oracle.

The bearing of the tunnel is 300 degrees, that is to say, towards the Heliacal sunset on June 21st, and the tunnel passes exactly under the Inner Sanctuary. The point where the roof reaches the water is exactly under the east wall of the Sanctuary. Whether there is any significance in this is not known.

Originally our first check in our explorations was at this landing. The foul atmosphere, heat and dust were not conducive to meticulous examination of our surroundings. We took coloured photographs by flashlight, and studied these later on the wall at home. In this way we found the tile in the roof over the beginning of the water, through which Keith climbed to pioneer the next stage. We cleared the dog-leg passage of the Rise, and found it to follow three sides of a square, to reach the hole covered by the tile. Further progress was still blocked because of earth filling, so we raked the earth from the steep Rise down

I

through the tile hole, until we had cleared a way to the top.

At this time we were of opinion that the Rise had been a mere escape route for the masons who had blocked the Inner Sanctuary. Recalling that we were undoubtedly the first people to penetrate to the water since the Oracle had been buried 2,000 years ago, we could not account for some broken walls at the landing. They seemed to have enclosed a square ante-chamber to the water. But there is no rubble on the ground to account for their broken appearance. In the Rise, we found evidence of a frame for a wooden door and we now consider the broken walls as probable supports for some woodwork which has completely disappeared in the course of the ages. This was an ante-chamber of some kind.

The level of the water is some 15 feet above tide level and the general water table in the ruins. There is no sign of an outlet, yet there must be a constant replacement for the water to remain clear and fresh. This is another of the unsolved mysteries.

Elsewhere in the ruins are some other springs. Behind the Piscina of Mercury is a remarkable spring which, one week, flows abundantly, discharging many hundreds of gallons of boiling water an hour. The very next week, there is a miserable trickle of cold water. At times, it stops altogether and the bowl of the spring becomes a horrible seething, squirming mass of mosquito larvae. Immediately below the Sacred Area is the large Piscina marked on the plan of Section III. Here is the 'Sorgente della Rogna'. The word 'rogna', is Italian for 'mange'. The spring is a strong solution of sulphur salts in cold water. The locals bring all the mangy dogs and scabious children, to take the waters.

None of these other springs is connected with the water of the Styx as we proved by using fluorescein. We feel quite justified in agreeing with Ephorus that "There is a fountain of potable water at sea level, but the people refrain from its use as they consider it to be the River Styx."

Having cleared sufficient earth from the Rise, to enable us to scramble up, we were now able to proceed. The Rise is 4 feet wide by an unknown height which by deduction we estimate at six to seven feet. It rises 20 feet from the landing and is 36 feet long. The section from the tile-hole to the top is 30 feet, and half-way up the bearing changes from 300 degrees to 285 degrees, thus effectively concealing from view, what is at the top.

Later we proved that the Rise is a stairway.

As we mount the Rise, the bend to 285 degrees is reached, and we see before us a flat level landing about three feet wide. At the far side is a rough wall, with what seems to be a blocked door on the left. Beginning at the door, and forming a shelf on the left of the Rise, is the start of the 120 passages. When the landing is reached, it is found to be a passage leading round to the right (north). The length of the rubble wall including the blocked door is just over four yards, and significantly, its bearing is 330 degrees. At the north corner it turns through a right angle towards the west, to end three yards further on against another blocked door. The details can be followed on the plan, Fig. 7. At right angles to this second door, in the rubble wall, is a third blocked door, opposite which there is a small antechamber, continuing towards the north, in a passage which, almost immediately turns in a semi-circle to the west. Then the roof of this passage descends steeply to the floor which is level. On further inspection the floor is seen to be rubble 'fill'. We lowered one of our party down a hole at the far end of this passage and we are satisfied, that it is really a filled up stair leading up from the far landing at the water below.

A block has fallen out of the filling in the second door, and we could see through into the interior of the space. It had obviously been filled right up to the roof. Natural settlement over the centuries has left a space between the fill and the roof of about a foot. We could see over more than half of the interior. Photographs revealed that the fill ceased, at the centre line of the room. We crawled in later and found it to be very similar in shape to the Etruscan house temples at Tarquinia, dating from the sixth to fifth centuries B.C.

The reconstruction was then simple, the rubble wall had been built by Agrippa's masons to reduce the size of the space to be filled, and the 'Doors' were their service entrances. In the front wall on the east side, the base of a column can be traced. The chamber consisted of a central rectangular space surrounded by supporting columns, which permitted an additional cloister, a yard wide. There were no doors at all. Entry from the stair from the far landing, could not be seen by a person coming

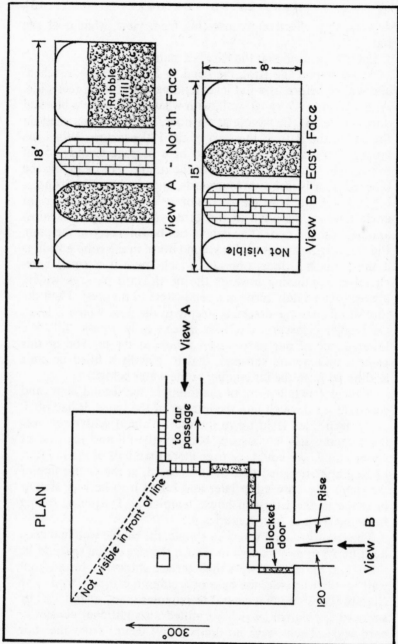

Fig. 7. The Inner Sanctuary

up, until the semicircular turn in the passage had been passed. On the east side the sharp change of direction in the Rise served the same purpose of disguise.

Surely we were justified in accepting this as the reference by Ephorus indicated, "they made their living by admitting strangers to the Sanctuary, situated far underground".

Outside the north blockage, in the little ante-chamber, there is a large niche low down at the floor, in addition to lamp niches and torch niches. Again, we feel justified in noting this low niche, as the vase for the offering of mistletoe or other flowers.

Opposite the south-east door blockage, a short shelf alongside the Rise, enters a passage some two feet wide and eight feet high. When we found it, it was completely filled with earth. On clearing sufficiently to pass over, it was found to divide at a point, about twenty feet from the blocked door. One section goes straight on at the level of the shelf. There is a short traverse, which opens into another and similar parallel passage, the roof of which is approximately six feet above that of its twin. These are the North 120 and the South 120. The same technique for smoke disposal has been provided as at the Dividing of the Ways, by fitting a door system in a wedge shaped space. The reason for the extra roof height in the North 120 is, in our opinion to ensure the diversion of the smoke into that passage for the purposes of ventilation. For some reason, the whole length of the North 120 has been filled with earth right up to the roof. Why? We were, in consequence, unable to traverse the North 120, but as with the Inner Sanctuary, the fill had settled with the passing of the years, by shining a light from either end, we were able to establish continuity and measure a change of bearing in the centre. At the east end the North 120 finishes behind the line of tiles in the roof of 290, at the Dividing of the Ways. The South 120 is approximately parallel to its northern counterpart. At the western end of this there is an earth blockage 20 feet long right up to the roof. There is a second blockage 20 feet long at 80 feet from the beginning at the traverse, and a change of bearing to correspond with that of the North 120 and to bring the tunnel to the junction with the 20 feet long extension of 270, behind the wall at the Dividing of the Ways. At the east end, there is a third earth blockage 20 feet long.

In the traverse between the two 120's at the west end, we found some graffiti. In letters a foot high and an inch wide, is roughly painted on the east wall, the word '*Illius*', and the conventional shorthand sign for a prayer to Hera. The graffitti are reproduced in Fig. 8, as they are difficult to photograph, owing to their position in the tunnel.

Alongside the graffiti in a lamp niche, we found a mason's lead plumb bob.

On the shelf at the commencement of the 120s, we found two lumps of solidified mortar, bearing the imprint of the baskets in which they were carried. The baskets have disintegrated and disappeared, but comparison of the weave and dimensions, showed that they were precisely similar to those still used to this day by the Italian builder's labourer for the same purpose. What intrigued us was finding them at all. How did it come about, that the overseer of the slaves allowed them to go out and leave these baskets. We always wonder if it were not an earthquake that caused them to panic and run for their lives.

In their length, the 120s rise about twenty feet from the floor of the Inner Sanctuary to the Dividing of the Ways.

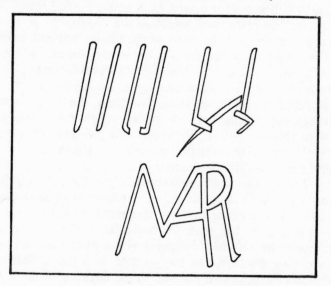

Fig. 8. GRAFFITI IN NORTH 120

There are several engineering problems that call for a little discussion. Was the whole complex as we see it built at one time, or was one section built first and the other later. If so, in what order was the work carried out? As now seen it bears all the evidence of a preconceived design. The orientation of the cliff face, towards the point of sunrise on Midsummer's day, the absolute accuracy of the bearing of 270° for 408 feet, the alignment of 290 and the 120s without any errors in the final junctions; finally the accurate orientation of the Inner Sanctuary towards the Helical Sunset, testify to an engineering skill of a high order.

Whether the 120 passages were built after the 290, or vice versa, there is quite a difficult problem in solid trigonometry to be solved. This involved the calculation of the horizontal angle and the dip or rise, necessary to reach the far end and effect a clean junction. What is more, this would have to be done before the work was started.

Another problem is the water. Did they know of the existence of this water, or did they find it by chance. Both views are equally possible.

One gets the impression that the 290 passage was built first, and that the Oracle, originally, may have consisted of the anteroom at the bottom of 290. In this manner, the ventilation would have been assured, as it is today. On the other hand, if the 120 passages (one of them), were considered to have formed with the Inner Sanctuary, the original Oracle, there seems no possibility of air circulation for ventilation purposes.

We think it certain that the work was designed, and was never a blind following of a fissure in the hillside, that emitted gas. Such a fissure would neither have the orientation, nor would it follow a straight course. This hypothesis can be dismissed.

Ephorus states that the original Oracle was destroyed "by a certain king", who did not like the answer to his questions. I think there is another explanation, which would account for the removal from the previous site (if indeed, it was moved). The last great eruption of Eponomeo on the Island of Ischia took place about 500 B.C., the date being well established by references in Greek writers. This was accompanied by a tremendous earthquake, that destroyed all the habitations in the

Phlegrean Fields and spread panic amongst the people. This was the 'king' that destroyed the Oracle, and it was reconstructed at Baiae. This explanation does not preclude the Oracle having been at Baiae all the time.

Having given a detailed description of the Sacred Area at Baiae, I can now collate the various items of evidence, upon which we base our claim, that here is the Oracle of the Dead.

1. Its situation, surrounded by the Cimmerian tunnels and *argillae* as described by Homer in the *Odyssey*.
2. The provision of the lamp niches, where there are none in all the other tunnels or *argillae*. The distribution of the lamp niches with 120 in the 408 feet of the entrance tunnel, 270, then no fewer than 400 set only a yard apart, in the inner 480 feet of galleries. This was not accidental, but is clear evidence that greater illumination and possibly more smoke effects, were desired in the inner recesses of the Oracle.
3. The clear evidence of technical design, and the fine workmanship in the cutting of the tunnels, the shape and dimensions being maintained very accurately.
4. The Inner Sanctuary corresponds with the reference by Ephorus and its similarity to the Etruscan house temples of the same date.
5. The suppression by Agrippa. The Inner Sanctuary was completely filled with earth. The stair up from the far landing was also filled to the level of the Sanctuary floor, a vertical rise of 20 feet. The Rise was similarly blocked, the length being 40 feet with the dog-leg. The bed of the water, also has been filled with rubble to a depth of at least 4 feet. The entire length of the North 120 was completely filled, throughout its 180 feet length. Three 20 foot long blocks were erected in South 120.
6. This was a tremendous operation. The 270 entrance tunnel is only 21 inches wide and there is no room for persons to pass anywhere except at the Dividing of the Ways. All this filling material was carried in from the surface in baskets. Calculation shows that some 700 cubic yards of earth were required for the work. The basket would hold about 40-50 pounds. No fewer than 30,000 man journeys were involved in the transport of all this material. The figures speak for themselves. They imply that Agrippa attached paramount importance to the operation. Why did he not just block the entrance to 270 under the temple? It seems certain that there was some psychological reason for doing the job the way he did.

6. The Oracle must have been a centre of pilgrimage. This requires a town to give the necessary supporting services, lodging, provision of food and sacrificial animals, with all the other incidentals of such activity. Nowhere in the vicinity of Avernus, except at Baiae is there such a town.

7. The 270 Entrance tunnel commences at the north-west corner of the temple. This was the quadrant of the ancient Cosmos, traditionally sacred to the Fates and the Deities of the Nether Regions. The significance is found in the famous bronze Liver found in an Etruscan tomb at Piacenza, which is an exposition of the Rules for Divination, as practised about the fourth century B.C.

8. The smoke control systems at the Dividing of the Ways and at the west end of the 120 is sound engineering practice. The whole idea of utilising convection as the key to the ventilation of a single entry tunnel complex, and the differential slopes that were used to ensure correct evacuation of the smoke and foul air in the desired direction, is evidence of preconceived design, for a purpose other than the mere clarifying of the passages from smoke. It was desired to send the streams of smoke in certain directions. Thus the line of tiles in the beginning of the roof of 290 is explained. The large volume of hot air travelling out along the roof of the North 120 and into the roof of 290, would not only ensure that the incoming cold air could maintain a breathable atmosphere in the lower part of the passages, but also go down the 290 stair quite freely to complete the ventilation circuit. Even today when only the 290 passage is in operation the ventilation is sufficient to allow short periods of work round the Inner Sanctuary. When the 120 doors were in use the system would be quite efficient.

9. The water is clearly also a part of the design. But how it was located and reached by the constructors, either by (a) the 290 stair, or (b) the 120s and the stairs down from the Sanctuary is an intriguing problem. There is no apparent outlet to the surface for the water, whereby its presence could be inferred. Its constant level and 'freshness' indicate some kind of flow, but we have been unable to find any solution to these problems. Whichever way it was reached, there are trigonometrical problems of some delicacy to be solved, and solved before work was started. The water was a part of the design, as may be deduced from the steps at the bottom of 290, the orientation of the water to pass directly under the Inner Sanctuary, namely 300 degrees.

10. The orientation of the cliff face towards the midsummer sunrise at North 60 degrees East, and that of the Inner Sanctuary towards the corresponding sunset, may have significance.

The details of the surface buildings, are not only difficult to recover, but they are doubtless of a very different date from the Oracle complex. Nevertheless they clearly form a self-contained architectural unit, and to that extent offer supporting evidence of the importance of the tunnel. The following are the details and measurements of the buildings on the Sacred Area. Reference to the plans and photographs will assist in their decipherment.

Commencing from the northern limit, the level is seen to be 6 feet above the general level of the wide flat space of Section III, the buildings on which are at a different orientation, namely 34 degrees.

Coming up the steps from Section III, the first building we call the Painted Room. This room has been reconstructed by the Italian authorities. When first excavated, the alcove at the west end of this room was blocked by a tufa wall, and its existence was not suspected. One day a block fell out of the wall, and the alcove was then cleaned up. Why was it sealed off? It seems to have been hidden at the time the main conversions were carried out. Yet when the wall was removed, all that could be seen, on the west wall, was the bare central panel surrounded by faint traces of decoration in the fourth Pompeian style.

We examined the bare panel, and photographed it with all coloured filters and even infra-red, yet there is no trace of any design on it. Moreover the surface has the appearance of having been rasped over with pumice or other abrasive, which has removed the top surface of the stucco and any painted design that it had upon it. The disappearance of painting by normal process of time can be discounted, because immediately beneath the central panel is a beautifully preserved painting of an Asphodel. Maybe this is an indication that, upon the panel was some painting of special significance, that even after its destruction by abrasion, still left an aura of mystery that necessitated closure of the alcove. The remainder of the walls bear traces of painting and designs. Also below the central panel at the west end is a shallow trench in the mosaic floor about one inch deep and ten inches wide, delineated by a thin white marble border, and lined with lines of black and yellow mosaic. The Painted Room measures 22 feet east-west by 12 feet 6 inches wide. There is a probe hole high up in the west wall, but we were assured by the excavators that there is no other room between this and the north tank behind and above. There is a marble doorstep, said to be in situ in the south wall, with the door cardinal. This opening seems to have been the communication between the Painted Room and the Big 'D'. To the east, there is a wide opening leading out on to a forecourt. On the north side of this is the arch already referred to, with steps leading down to Section III. The forecourt floor was originally covered with vari-coloured marble tiles. In the south-west corner are four broken marble blocks, which appear to be the legs of a table or perhaps an altar, upon which the augurs examined the victims. Looking out eastwards, Vesuvius is seen in the distance. The floor of the forecourt is 22 feet 6 inches east-west by 17 feet 6 inches wide. In the east wall is a large 'D' shaped bath and a similar, but smaller one in the south wall.

Next to the Painted Room is the Big 'D'. In front of the cliff face is a space 20 feet square. The 'D' which is cut into the cliff was converted into a hot room with a hypocaust floor. It lies entirely within the cliff. We think that before conversion, it was the apse of some kind of chapel, or perhaps the apse where some important statue stood. At the side of the 'D', there is a statue niche, which on close examination reveals that it hides the entrance to a stairway, as the two lines of stucco which covered the passage walls are visible at the sides of the niche. Just at the rear of the niche, and opening on to the 'D' is a hole about eighteen inches square made by a grave-robber. We went in here and found ourselves at the bottom of a steep stair, leading upwards and later found to finish against the wall of the south tank. This stair is 2 feet wide and 6 feet in height. At the top is trace of another passage at right angles, that may have connected with the north tank.

Although the wall footings jutting out from the cliff face towards the east are very much damaged and only two or three feet high, something can be learnt from them. For example there are numerous stopped up openings, where the tufa blocks contrast with the *opus reticulatum* of the wall. We can thus deduce that there were entrances in to the buildings from the east. By the same reasoning, there was no connection between the Big 'D' and the Sudatorium, which is the next building to the south.

The open space in front of the Sudatorium, measures in common with all the walls, 20 feet to the east boundary wall, by 13 feet wide. The lower entrance is 3 feet 9 inches wide by about 7 feet high, with a square light shaft above. The remarkable feature is, that the entrance is neither central with the forecourt, or with the interior. The Sudatorium as seen today presents a reconstruction of a Roman 'hot-room', with its typical raised hypocaust floor, upon ceramic supports which allowed the hot air to circulate under the floor and heat it. The hot air was brought into the room by means of the passage at the rear. This passage connects with the 270 entrance tunnel. At the junction there is a wall blockage, through which there is a circular hole. This is the hole referred to previously, through which the terracotta pipe passed, bringing the hot gas from the orifice lower down the slope, in through the trench under the temple. The Sudatorium is a circular, bottle-shaped building 16 feet in diameter by 16 feet high, with a 3 feet diameter circular vent at the top. This vent opens on to the terrace level above. The interior of the building is lined with Neronian brickwork, which is badly cracked and the plan of the building is no longer truly circular, owing to pressure of the overlying structures. The rim of the vent is provided with four white marble blocks which appear to have been supports for some kind of cover. This would leave a space between the cover and the rim of about nine inches. Under the floor of the Sudatorium is a passage. The arch of the entrance is still there, so that the original dimensions can be seen. The passage extends for 32 feet on a bearing of 245 degrees until it joins the main 270 tunnel. Although today, we see Neronian brickwork lining the Sudatorium, this is probably due to repair after the great earthquake of A.D. 63. But the presence of this circular building in a setting composed of obvious conversions, does not seem quite in keeping. We are of opinion that this building is one of the oldest of the surface group.

The next building to the south we designate the Original Entrance. The forecourt is only 8 feet wide, and at one time had a raised hypocaust floor. The silhouette is interesting as it comprises a tufa masonry wall, into which iron sprags were driven to act as a support for a facing of decorated stucco, a portion of which remains in the upper left hand corner of the vault. The floor has been partly excavated to reveal that, in front of this decorated panel was a vaulted recess 3 feet in depth. Above this and 6 feet higher up is another silhouette of a vault, which formed the roof to the whole.

At the bottom of the vault is the entrance to a passage. This bears evidence of at least three reconstructions of very different dates. The passage eventually joins the 270 tunnel at a point 5 feet 3 inches west of the smoke face. Between the north wall of the Original Entrance and 270 is all artificial construction, including the Grotto above the 270, and some chambers leading off the Grotto, lying above the Original Entrance passage. There is a blockage 5 feet in from the face of the vault and behind this there is a considerable change of direction of the passage to the junction with 270. The photograph shows the several reconstructions at the entrance to this passage, better than any written description. The reason for this complicated layout is a matter of speculation. It does appear, however, from the appearance of the outer south wall of the temple, that at one time, the temple stood proud of the cliff face by about eight feet. This, the rear wall of the temple, corresponds in line with the rear of the blockage in the passage of the Original Entrance, behind which there is a small enlarged space. But all speculation does not account for the great amount of fill and reconstruction, that there is in this immediate area. What one tends to forget, is that a considerable amount of timber was used in building construction, by the Etruscans and other Italiote tribes. This has all perished with the years and leaves problems of reconstruction that are impossible of solution.

There seems to have been no specific dividing line between the Original Entrance and the temple. The temple was originally a square, built entirely of ashlar blocks, each wall being 20 feet long. It is possible to trace a sub-structure of courses of blocks running north and south up to a level which may have been a floor. One is reminded of a similar form of floor support recently excavated at Paestum in an archaic temple. It supported a wooden floor. Apart from this, all is Roman construction dating from Augustan and Neronian times. At one point the ashlar blocks seems to hint at a stair down into the trench. The trench itself continues to the east; eventually coming to daylight in a room in Section IV. Traces of the courses of blocks can be seen in the concrete of the present south wall. It may be that the blocks had become dangerous as the result of an earthquake. They were used as a form against which to pour the concrete and then removed.

The original usage of the temple has been completely altered and the fittings converted to an unknown rite. We are not competent to make any suggestions on this.

In the west wall there is a hole leading to the Room of Memory, which I have suggested, may be the result of filling up of the former space between the rear wall of the temple and the cliff face, due to a former landslide. We were unable to trace the full length of the passage which leads out of the Room of Memory on a bearing of 282 degrees as it is filled with earth filling. We can see for a distance of about twenty feet, at which point it appears to widen out. We have suggested that eventually this passage connected with 270 at the point where the Sudatorium passage also joins.

Our claims as to what forms the Oracle of the Dead are solely in respect of the tunnel complex, the surface buildings may or may not be of an equally ancient original date.

The ten items I have listed above seem to us strong evidence of the soundness of our deductions. Any observations I have made about the surface buildings may offer support but we do not consider them vital to the main issue.

If the archaeological world accepts our claim to have identified the Oracle of the Dead at Baiae, a new field of research is open. In spite of meagre references in Roman writers, it ought to be possible, greatly to extend our knowledge of the cultural role played by Baiae at the beginning of our era.

Keith and I feel we have made a worthwhile contribution at the smallest estimate, and one of considerable importance if our proofs are valid and acceptable.

Owing to the generally rough surfaces with which the measurements are concerned, we consider our standard of accuracy is of the order of 2 per cent $\pm$ in lengths and levels and 2 degrees $\pm$ in angular distances. The thickness of walls is specially difficult, as in some cases it is not easy to determine if they were faced with stucco or not. 'Weight' and the tendency of the cliff face to slip towards the east, has caused ellipticity in the Sudatorium, and deviation from the rectilinear in the south tank. The amount of debris and calcareous deposit on the floor of the passages, must vary from point to point and our dimensions for these are therefore estimates of the average.

In spite of all the agencies acting over many centuries, such as earthquakes, water seepage, human vandals, the underground complex is in a remarkable state of preservation.

We apologise for the poor condition of the photographs of some of the underground views. We hasten to say that this is not entirely our bad technique. The state of the atmosphere must be allowed for. The thick dust laden air makes the pictures look out of focus. The lack of contrast in the drab walls of the tunnels sometimes give the impression of over exposure. Remembering these little details will perhaps add to the sense of the dramatic when looking at the records of this wonderful place.

5

Ritual in the Oracle

There is nothing in the world today that compares in any way with the ancient Oracles. They were a product of the mental evolution of the times. Before 'scientific method' came to be the normal accepted way of solving unknown problems, all such events were ascribed to the supernatural.

It should not be lightly assumed that all the exponents of the art of divination as practised at the Oracles were ignorant charlatans. The belief in the divine origin of auguries, omens and even dreams, was so deeply ingrained in the minds of the people, that obviously the diviners also were convinced that they were truly interpreting the Divine Will.

Dreams were specially important. In St. Matthew's Gospel, there are several instances. In Chapter II we read, that when the Magi came to worship the new-born Child, they were in some danger of arrest by the authorities, "and being warned of God in a dream, that they should not return to Herod, they departed into their own country another way. And when they were departed, behold the angel of the Lord appeareth to Joseph in a dream, saying, Arise and take the young Child and his Mother and flee into Egypt."[1]

Another famous example is the false dream sent by Zeus to Agamemnon, as a punishment for his treatment of Achilles. Agamemnon dreamed that if he attacked the Trojans the next day he would inflict the final defeat. On awakening, he called together the War Council of the Greek leaders, and told them of his dream. They agreed unanimously, that such a direct message from Zeus should not be ignored, but must be obeyed. The *Iliad* tells the story of the disastrous defeat of the Greeks that ensued.[2]

144

The River Styx . . . a placid expanse of limpid water 200 yards
inside the wall of the Crater of Avernus and 150 feet below the
surface of the earth. Greek writers say the only thing that can
resist the corrosive action of the water is a horse's hoof. Yet the
author and his friends dived in it and drank it and are all still
without ill effect.

(*Left*) Keith Jones standing on the site of the ancient altar made of ash and bone. (*Right*) David Lewis at the edge of the River Styx, where he made his spectacular dive with Robert Love.

Omens were equally held in awe. The Roman historian Suetonius, writes in his *Lives of the Twelve Caesars*, of the signs preceding the death of the Emperor Domitian.

Throughout his reign, Domitian had made a practice of commending each new year to the care of the Goddess Fortune at Palestrina, and each year she had granted him the same favourable omen. But this year the omen was a dreadful one, portending bloodshed. Domitian also dreamed that Minerva, whom he worshipped fervently, emerged from her shrine to tell him she had been disarmed by Jupiter and could no longer protect him. What disturbed him most, however, was a prediction by the astrologer Ascletarion and its sequel. This man when charged, made no secret of having revealed the future, which he had foreseen by magical means. Domitian at once asked whether he could prophesy the manner of his own end, and upon Ascletarion's replying that he would very soon be torn to pieces by dogs, had him executed on the spot, and gave orders that the funeral should be conducted with the greatest care, as a further proof that all magicians lied. But while the funeral was in progress a sudden gale scattered the pyre and a pack of stray dogs mangled the astrologer's half-burned corpse. Latinus, the comic actor, who happened to witness the incident, mentioned it at a dinner when he brought Domitian the latest city gossip.[3]

Before undertaking any operation or journey of any importance, the augur was always consulted. The sea voyage was a venture into the unknown, that required the most careful religious preparation. Sacrifices were made to the god of the desired wind, and the augur made certain that the sacrifices had been favourably received by the god, before the ship sailed. On the bows of the ship, eyes were painted, so that she could see where she was going. This practice is still common in the Mediterranean. During the voyage offerings were made to the gods of the sea. The most unfortunate circumstance that could happen to a ship was that there should be a jinx on board, either in the crew or amongst the passengers. Remember the story of Jonah in the Bible. Jonah took ship at Joppa to go to Tarshish. On the voyage a great storm blew up and frightened the crew of the vessel, who began to pray to their gods and search for the jinx who had caused the storm. Jonah apparently was seasick, and had gone below to sleep. The captain came to him and said,

K

Tell us, we pray thee, for whose cause this evil is upon us. What is thine occupation and whence comest thou, what is thy country and of what people art thou? And he said unto them, I am an Hebrew; and I fear the Lord, the God of Heaven, which hath made the sea and the dry land. Then were the men exceedingly afraid, and said unto him, why hast thou done this? For the men knew that he fled from the presence of the Lord for he had told them. Then said they unto him, what shall we do unto thee that the sea shall be calm unto us?, for the sea wrought and was tempestuous. And he said unto them, take me up and cast me forth into the sea, so shall the sea be calm unto you; for I know that for my sake this great tempest is upon you.

Quite apart from the aptness of the illustration of the belief in a jinx, this is a very human story. One can imagine poor seasick Jonah saying to the captain, I feel awful, leave me alone or throw me overboard, I just want to die.[4]

The diviner and the interpreter of dreams were the most important persons in the community. Divining was carried out in a variety of ways. Juvenal, in one of his amusing satires on life in ancient Rome, describes the visit of the Roman ladies to the fortune tellers and diviners in the city markets.

Here is the Armenian Augur, or one from Commargene, scratching in the lungs of a dead pigeon, still warm; guaranteeing a tender lover, or a huge legacy from a rich uncle with no children. He will look into the hearts of fowls, the guts of a pup, and perhaps on very special occasions, the entrails of a child; then he will be able to grant, whatever you wish. But you should rely more on the prognostications of the Chaldeans, as whatever they say is said to be the word of Jupiter Ammon himself.[5]

The Etruscans divined by inspecting the livers of the sacrifices. Some years ago a bronze model of a liver was found at Piacenza, inscribed with the basic rules for divination. The liver is divided into quadrants as a kind of celestial map. There is an equatorial line, bisected by a north-south line. Each quadrant has its special significance and each its dedication to its own deity. The north-eastern section is devoted to the Celestial Gods, Zeus, Athene, Apollo and the rest, the east end of the equator being sacred to Hera. The south-western quadrant belongs to Dionysius and the Earth. Due south is the Sun. The whole of the western Hemisphere is assigned to the less auspicious factors. The south-western quadrant is dedicated to the Fates, the north-west to the Underworld Gods, and the north Pole to Death.

The diviner imagined himself standing at the intersection of the equatorial and polar lines and facing south. Each quadrant was divided into sixteen sub-sections each with its appropriate influence. The flight of birds was often observed for the taking of omens, and was interpreted by readings of the liver. A flight coming in from the east was one of the best signs, especially if, when overhead, they turned and departed the same way. Conversely a flight from the west was fraught with evil and if they turned towards the north, a death was imminent.[6]

This system of quadrature in divination was soon applied to town planning as a means of ensuring the protection of the gods. The layout of Herculaneum is an excellent example. The north-south streets are called cardines, and the cross streets at right angles are decumani, the forum, the municipal buildings and the temples are concentrated at the main equatorial cross roads.

There were many Oracles in the ancient Mediterranean world, some three hundred in all, perhaps a dozen of which were important. In addition to their purely local functions of service to the population, these were consulted by strangers and even by foreign Governments. It follows that these principal Oracles had an incalculable influence on the evolution of civilisation and the political history of the region. By far the most influential was that at Delphi.

Croesus, King of Lydia, was the richest and most powerful ruler of his day, when he was master of the whole of western Asia Minor. The River Halys was the frontier between his dominions and the growing power of the Persian Empire under Cyrus. Croesus considered whether he should attack the Persians before they got too strong. "He accordingly sent emissaries to the Oracles in Greece and Lybia, and sent different persons to different places, some to Delphi, some to Abae of Phocis and some to Dordona; others were sent to Amphiaraus and Trophonius, and others to Branchidae of Milesia; these were the Grecian Oracles to which Croesus sent to consult. He sent others also to consult that of Ammon in Lybia." In due course a similar reply was received from each, to the effect that "if Croesus attacked the Persians he would destroy a great Empire". With this favourable omen, Croesus crossed over the River Halys and attacked the Persians at Pteria. The result of the battle was indecisive, but as winter was approaching and the snow on the Anatolian highlands was making campaigning impossible, Croesus withdrew his army to his capital, Sardis, and disbanded all his forces. Cyrus anticipated this move and made a forced march with his cavalry, thus catching Croesus completely unprepared. He was able to storm the city with ease. A great Empire was indeed destroyed . . . that of Croesus himself.

Most of the answers of the Oracles were ambiguous, so that whatever occurred as a result of following their advice, they were always right.[7]

It is impossible for us to realise the tremendous influence these Oracles had on the march of civilisation. However the ritual for receiving the divine message was performed in public, there must have been a committee of extremely wise political experts to ensure a rational interpretation which would be acceptable to the enquirers. That of Dordona was the oldest, but the famous Oracle at Delphi soon became the most important and influential in the whole of the eastern Mediterranean. Originally it had belonged to the Great Goddess who came to Greece with the first migrants from Lybia. Her symbol was the *omphalos*, or navel. This sacred object was considered the centre of the whole world and it has survived to this day. It was a stone allegory of the domestic hearth, a conical stone, originally coloured black, red and white to represent a charcoal fire.[8] The Oracle itself seems to have been given in an underground room, by a priestess called the Pythoness. The serpent Python had belonged to the Great Moon Goddess. When Apollo seized the shrine, he killed the serpent and its mate that gave the Oracles. This action so incensed the local population that the priests of Zeus were disturbed at the unrest. Zeus ordered that Apollo should institute Annual Games in memory of the serpents at which he should preside; further that the Priestess of the Oracle should be called the Pythoness. The Pythoness sat upon a tripod, and inhaled fumes from a brazier underneath. The fire was fed with Indian hemp, ivy, laurel (bay), and rosemary. As the fumes began to take effect, the burblings that the Pythoness uttered, were translated by a commission of priests into the answers required by the suppliants.

The Romans considered the Oracles at Baiae and at Cuma as equal in importance to that of Delphi, and they apparently continued to consult them as late as the fourth century A.D.

The method of consultation at the different Oracles varied. At Delphi all that was necessary was to send a gift commensurate with the import of the question, and the Pythoness would give an answer. At Dordona, and also at the Oracle of Ammon in Lybia, the priestesses interpreted the cooing of doves and the rustling of the leaves in the grove of oak trees.

On the other hand, at the Oracle of Trophonius there was considerable personal discomfort and even risk, in the consultation. In some respects the Oracle at Baiae and that of Trophonius resemble each other, and a description of a visit to consult Trophonius should help to reconstruct the rites at Baiae. Pausanias visited the Oracle of Trophonius at Labadeia in Greece, and as usual has left a wonderful story of his experiences.

Just as we expect to find the church services at the church that we attend, to be the same in whatever church of the same denomination that we enter, I think the same can be said of the temples of Apollo, whether these temples were in Greece, or Italy, or elsewhere. In the same way the technique employed at one Oracle may well have been employed at another. Keith and I think there were similarities in the procedure at Labadeia and at Baiae, which all help to prove our claims, and incidentally help in reconstructing the rites at Baiae. The Oracle at Labadeia seems to have been given by a serpent. But as in all Greek descriptions of the Mysteries, just at the critical moment when things begin to get really interesting, and we hope to get the culmination of the rites, the narrator says, "what follows, it is unlawful for me to disclose to the uninitiated". But even so, Pausanias tells a thrilling story.

The most famous things in the Grove are a temple and an image of Trophonius. The image made by Praxiteles, is after the likeness of Aesclepius. There is also a sanctuary of Demeter surnamed Europa, and a Zeus Rain-God in the open. If you go up to the Oracle, and thence onwards up the mountain, you come to what is called the Maid's Hunting, and a Temple of King Zeus.

This temple they have left half-finished, either because of its size or the long succession of wars. In a second temple there are the images of Cronos, Hera and Zeus. There is also a Sanctuary of Apollo.

What happens at the Oracle is as follows. When a man has made up his mind to descend to the Oracle of Trophonius, he first lodges in a certain building for an appointed number of days, this being sacred to the Good Spirit and to Good Fortune. While he lodges there, among other regulations for purity, he abstains from hot baths, bathing only in the River Hercyna. Meat he has in plenty from the sacrifices, for he who descends to Trophonius, sacrifices to Trophonius himself and to the children of Trophonius, to Apollo also and to Cronos, to Zeus surnamed King, to Hera Charioteer, and to Demeter, whom they surname Europa, and say was the nurse of Trophonius. At each sacrifice a diviner is present, who looks into the entrails of the victim, and after inspection, prophesies to the person descending whether Trophonius will give him a kind and gracious reception. The entrails of the other victims do not declare the mind of Trophonius so much as a ram, which each enquirer sacrifices over a pit on the night he descends, calling upon Agamedes. Even though the previous sacrifices have appeared propitious, no account is taken of them, unless the entrails of the ram indicate the same. But if they agree, the enquirer descends in good hope.

The procedure of the descent is this. First, during the night, he is taken to the River Hercyna by two boys of the citizens about thirteen years old, named Hermae, who after taking him there, anoint him with oil and wash him. It is these who wash the descender, and do all the other necessary things as his attendant boys. After this he is taken by the priests, not at once to the Oracle, but to fountains of water very near to each other. Here he must drink water called the Water of Forgetfulness that he may forget all he has been thinking of hitherto, and afterwards, he drinks of another water, the Water of Memory, which causes him to remember what he sees after his descent. After looking at the image, which they say was made by Daedalus (it is not shown by the priests, save to those who are going to visit Trophonius). Having seen it and worshipped it and prayed, he proceeds to the Oracle, dressed in a linen tunic with ribbons girding it and wearing the boots of the country.

The Oracle is on the mountain beyond the Grove. Round it is a circular basement of white marble, the circumference of which is about that of the smallest threshing floor, while its height is just short of two cubits. On the basement stand spikes, which like the crossbars holding them together, are of bronze, while through them has been made a double door. Within the enclosure is a chasm in the earth, not natural, but constructed after the most accurate masonry. The shape of its structure is like that of a bread oven. Its breadth across the middle, one might conjecture to be about four cubits, and its depth also could not be estimated to extend to more than eight cubits. They have made no way of descent to the bottom, but when a man comes to Trophonius, they bring him a narrow light ladder. After going down, he finds a hole between the floor and the structure. Its breadth appears to be two spans and its height one span. The descender lies with his back on the ground, holding barley cakes kneaded with honey, thrusts his feet into the hole and himself follows, after trying hard to get his knees into the hole. After his knees, his body is at once swiftly drawn in, just as the largest and most rapid river will catch a man in its eddy and draw him under. After this, those who have entered the shrine learn the future, not in one and the same way in all cases, but by sight sometimes, at others by hearing.

The return upwards is by the same route, the feet darting out first. They say, that no one who has made the descent has been killed, save only the bodyguard of Demetrius, but they declare that he performed none of the rites in the sanctuary and that he descended, not to consult the god, but in the hope of stealing gold and silver from the shrine. It is said, that the body of this man appeared in a different place, and was not cast out at the sacred mouth. Other tales are told about the fellow, but I have given the one more worthy of consideration. After his ascent from Trophonius, the enquirer is again taken in hand by the priests, who set him upon a chair called the Chair of Memory, which stands not far from the shrine. They ask of him, when seated there, all that he has seen and learned. After gaining this information, they entrust him to his relatives. These lift him, paralysed with terror and unconscious both of himself and of his surroundings, and carry him to the building where he lodged before with Good Fortune and the Good Spirit.

Afterwards, however, he will recover all his faculties, and the power to laugh will return to him. What I write is not hearsay; I have myself, enquired of Trophonius and seen other enquirers.

Those who have descended into the shrine of Trophonius are obliged to dedicate a tablet, on which is written all that they have heard, or seen. The Shield of Aristomenes is also preserved here; its story I have already given in a former part of my works.

This Oracle was once unknown to the Boeotians. But they learned of it in the following way. As there had been no rain for a year and more, they sent to Delphi, envoys from each city. They asked for a cure for the drought, and were bidden by the Pythoness to go to Trophonius at Lebadeia to discover the remedy from him. Coming to Lebadeia, they could not find the Oracle. Thereupon Saon, one of the envoys from the city of

Acraephnium and the oldest of them all, saw a swarm of bees. It occurred to him to follow wherever the bees turned. At once he saw the bees flying into the ground here, and he went with them into the Oracle. It is said, that Trophonius taught Saon the customary ritual, and all the observances kept at the Oracle.[9]

We tend to forget that in ancient times the patriarchal and the feudal systems of society meant that wealth and power was concentrated into the hands of very few people. Most writings that have survived to us deal with the lives and deeds of aristocrats and the upper middle class. Nevertheless there must have been a lower middle class of independent persons, such as small shopkeepers, traders and artisans together with the more senior employees of the 'big house'. All the remainder were serfs and slaves. Slaves amongst the Greeks were treated even worse than their companions in misery under the Romans. They were considered solely as items of property; they had no rights as human beings. They were on a par with the farm animals, and their owners were not, in the slightest degree, interested in their religion, their thoughts, or their feelings. The slaves were so numerous as to constitute a grave problem of social security. The main reason why they did not revolt and overwhelm their masters was their diversity of origin, which prevented any corporate action or unity.

Yet the indolence of the aristocrat, both Greek and Roman, permitted the more intelligent of the slaves to appropriate the management of their owner's affairs, acquiring riches in the process. Eventually they were emancipated and became the class of 'Freedmen' about which so much is written by such historians as Tacitus and Suetonius. Several Freedmen actually became Ministers to the Caesars, Narcissus to Claudius, Anicetus as Admiral to Nero. All these men would continue to worship their national gods, even perhaps whilst outwardly paying service to Jupiter. In this way the seeds of Christianity that came to Baiae via Puteoli, found fertile soil amongst the slaves in the great villas. In two or three centuries the new religion had conquered the Roman Empire.

The Oracles were generally associated with a Sanctuary of Apollo, who was also the god of medicine. Thus the Oracle was also the community centre of the town. Apart from its spectacular function of guiding the policies of States, and the consultations of dead relatives by wealthy aristocrats, there were many other essential functions that it peformed.

I have already referred to the need for obtaining favourable omens, before setting out on a journey, or beginning any important operation. The diviners at the Oracle dealt with all these requests, doubtless on payment of a suitable fee.

Belief in witchcraft was also absolute. The Oracle was therefore in much demand for counter spells to remove the disease that some enemy had wished on the pig or the cow. All illnesses were accounted for by the victim having been 'overlooked' by a witch. Even today, in this village where I live near Baiae, there are many mothers who take their children, with whooping cough, or some other childish complaint, first to the *strega* and then to the doctor. I have a feeling they have more faith in the witch than in the doctor.

Love potions were also a profitable source of revenue. Juvenal, in his satires, cynically remarks, that many women reduced their husbands and lovers to physical wrecks by the horrible mixtures they gave them to arouse their passions.

Every morning there was a long procession, especially of women, to have their dreams interpreted. Many of these beliefs and customs still survive in Southern Italy, probably as a tradition from Magna Grecia which has never died out. In every village there is the Banco del Lotto, the Receiving Office for the weekly National Lottery. This is a numbers game similar to 'Bingo'. Bets can be made upon combinations of two, three, four, or five numbers. The problem is to pick the right numbers. Here the ancient art of divination, and interpretation of dreams is appealed to. Every number from one to ninety has a meaning. Every chance situation can be expressed as one of these numbers, and the event is regarded as a direct message from the supernatural, to bet these numbers on the Lotto. A bank manager in Naples told me quite seriously, that he had dreamed, that he saw a large snake with a bird's head, eating a fish. He consulted the *Smorfie*, a wonderful book that gives the meaning and interpretation of such dreams, with the corresponding numbers for the Lotto. He decided to bet on the three numbers corresponding to snake, bird and fish, 89-7-18. He concluded his story woefully, "Snake and Fish turned up, the third number was 'Head, 77'. The possibility was obvious,

I should have covered it also." Even a bank manager can be wise after the event.

It is very amusing in the Banco del Lotto to hear some old woman say "the baby coughed all night and I heard a rat squeal outside on the stairs". The clerk solemnly suggests "I should bet on 'Baby's Cough', 'Running Rats' and 'Stairs'." The bet is duly made "Terno secco—26-36-43" is duly written on the ticket. And . . . of course these are winning numbers. As almost everyone who plays the Lotto relies on similar sources for their inspiration, the belief is firmly established that every large win is due to supernatural assistance.

Whether there was a Lotto at Baiae in Roman times, I have not found any evidence to show. But they played dice as I found one in the ruins there, and there are many specimens in the Naples Museum that came from Pompeii. Gambling and the eternal hope of getting something for nothing is part of the human make-up, and will never die out.

I feel that we should be quite in order, if we assume that the Oracle of the Dead and the Sanctuary of Apollo at Baiae, offered the major part of the services that were given by similar institutions elsewhere. Judging from the meagre evidence at our disposal, three stages of evolution can be traced.

We have three known dates when reference was made to the Oracle by historians or poets. Homer wrote in 800 B.C., Ephorus in 450 B.C. and Vergil in 30 B.C. We also know that Hannibal visited it in 209 B.C. There must have been an Oracle and the monastery of the Cimmerian priests at Baiae a considerable period before 800 B.C. for its fame to have spread to Asia Minor by that date. The first concept that the Phlegrean Fields were the site of the Entrance to the Underworld probably occurred to the very first explorers, awed by the sight of the devastation caused by the incessant volcanic activity. This may have been as long ago as 2500 B.C., with the coming of the Lybians from North Africa to Cuma and Paestum, when the bronze age with just beginning.[10] Even at this distant date the Egyptians already had large seaworthy ships depicted on their monuments. The Minoans of Crete and the Myceneans in Southern Greece were also maritime peoples sailing and exploring in every direction as far west as Spain and even down the west African coast. It is not inconceivable, that as soon as they had established a permanent settlement at Cuma, the Oracle began to be consulted. On the mainland of Greece, the Oracles were all pre-Hellenic, and were originally established in honour of the Great Earth Goddess. We know that in early Roman times, the Oracles at Baiae and Cuma, were held to be of comparable status with Delphi itself.

The voyage of Odysseus (Ulysses), would have taken place about 1180 B.C. immediately following the sack of Troy. This date is now well established, even more accurately than the date of Homer himself, who probably lived about 800 B.C., or it may have been 900 B.C. The difference is not important, the point is that he wrote the *Odyssey* about that date. In comparing his story with the voyage of Aeneas as told by Vergil a thousand years later, we are struck by certain obvious differences in detail, in the descriptions of the visits to the Baiae area.

Odysseus does not have to go first to consult the Sibyl at Cuma. In fact he did not go to Cuma at all.

Odysseus sacrificed only two animals, "a young ram and a black ewe" that Circe had given to him for the purpose. Aeneas on the other hand was obliged to provide, "seven oxen, not yet broken to the yoke and seven black ewes carefully chosen" as a sacrifice before he could consult the Sibyl. Then when they arrived at the Oracle he sacrificed "four black skinned young oxen to Hecate, a black lamb to Night, who is the Mother of the Furies and to Earth her sister, then a sterile cow to Persephone, and entire bulls to the Lord of the Underworld burnt on the sacred fire of the altar, covered with olive oil."

The cynic will say, this is a typical example of rising prices, when any activity becomes clothed with officialdom.

The whole story, as related first by Homer and then by Vergil, is full of interest. We learn how the concept of the Underworld, and life after death had progressed between the two dates.

Odysseus carried out a simple ceremony to call the Shades for consultation. Whilst Homer does not mention them, it seems certain that there must have been Cimmerian priests to instruct him how to proceed.[11] Further there is no mention of his actually going underground. Yet at the end of his visit, his Mother says to him, "It is time for you to hasten back to the

light of day." This seems to show that he was underground at
the time. I think this lack of information is due to two reasons.
In the first place, it is noticeable that Homer pays far less
attention to description of places than of people. Secondly,
Homer wrote from hearsay, and Vergil from eye-witness knowledge. Thirdly, the views on the aspect and constitution of the
Underworld had increased in complexity. In Homer's day
admission to the Elysian Fields was reserved for the very few,
sons of Gods and later Heroes.[12] The ordinary person just died
and his shade lived for ever as a shadowy wraith without any
personality, in the Meadow of Asphodel. The simple ceremony
of making a trench over which to sacrifice the victims and
collect their blood, was doubtless considered sufficient to recall
the Shade with a libation. It was a normal practice of devout
relatives to proceed to the tomb of the departed and there pour
a libation of blood to relieve the sufferings of the dead. The
description of the little ceremony runs, "around this trench
I poured libations to all the Dead, first with mingled honey and
milk, then with sweet wine, and last of all with water. Over
this I sprinkled some white barley, and then began my prayers
to the helpless ghosts of the Dead."[13] He drew his sword and
sat down by the trench, allowing none of the shades to
approach and drink of the blood until he saw Teiresias
approaching. Having had his conversation with the Seer and
also with his Mother, Odysseus continues, "I stuck to my post
in the hope, that I might yet be visited by other men who had
perished long ago. And now I should have gone still further
back in time and seen the heroes that I wished to meet, Theseus
for instance and Perithous, those glorious children of the gods.
But before that could happen, the tribes of the dead came up,
and gathered round me in their tens of thousands, raising their
eerie cry. Sheer panic turned me pale gripped by the sudden
fear that dread Persephone might send me up from Hades'
Halls some ghastly monster like the Gorgon's head. I made off
quickly to my ship."

In all Homer's poems there is a contrast between the rich
descriptions of his human characters and the sparse details of
the settings. Here also he gives practically no details of the
Oracle. "We reached the point that Circe had described." Circe
had said to him, "March on into Hades' Kingdom of Decay.

There a River of Flaming Fire and the River of Lamentation, which is a branch of the waters of the Styx, unite round a rock." This may be a hearsay description of the "Dividing of the Ways" in the Antrum of the Oracle and shows that Odysseus was instructed "to go *into* Hades Kingdom". The important difference in the two stories, is the absence of the Sybil from Homer. Pausanias, in his description of Delphi, gives a list of the Sibyls, including one who came from Cuma. But he gives no clue by which a date can be inferred. Ephorus writing in 450 B.C. also does not mention any Oracle or Sibyl at Cuma.[14] Whether it is safe to infer from this, that the Oracle at Cuma was founded after 500 B.C. is very doubtful. All that can be said is, that she was not in control of the Oracle in the time of Homer.[15]

When Ephorus wrote in 450 B.C., the Inner Sanctuary was already built, and in use. The Odyssey gives no help in this problem, except in a negative way. Even if it could be inferred that Odysseus went in as far as the Dividing of the Ways, there is nothing in the story to suggest that he went any further. Whether this adds any support to my previous hypothesis that the complex beyond this point may have been constructed at separate dates, is also open to question. Apparently in the time of Ephorus, there were no conspicuous surface buildings. There is a possibility that these had not yet been reconstructed after the disastrous earthquake connected with the eruption of Eponomeo, which must have occurred very shortly before this.

We come now to the time of Vergil. The speech of Anchises proves that Vergil was a devout Orphic, and the remainder of Book VI of the *Aeneid* is an elaborate exposition of Orphic beliefs. Times were dangerous. The civil war between Octavian and Antony was in full spate and any unguarded word could lead to arrest and execution. Although Vergil was a close friend of Octavian, he delayed publication of the *Aeneid* so long, that he died before it appeared. It was eventually published after his death, on the express orders of Augustus. Was the reason for this, the proscription by Agrippa of the Oracle for some religious reason. Although Vergil is obviously describing the galleries at Baiae, he does not mention them by name, or make the association too obvious. Keith and I have discussed many times the implication on our identification, of his description of the Fields of Joy, the Elysian Fields and the waters of Lethe; none of which can possibly be identified with anything in the galleries. These are Orphic concepts but very difficult to portray. In addition, remember, the Oracle had already been in existence for centuries before these concepts became fashionable. Orphism was a *religio licet*, that is, permitted by the authorities. It would therefore seem that there was something more than the rites of Apollo and Orphic practices, which caused the ruthless suppression by Agrippa. After the civil war was over and Augustus was Emperor, there was a period of literary and cultural revival which paralleled that of the Middle Ages. Augustus was a tolerant Caesar in this respect, and the Phlegrean Fields again became the exchange where Greek culture passed to Roman youth.

The general condition of the ruins at Baiae is such that it is impossible to assign the original purpose to any of them with any degree of certainty. Lower down the hillside in Section IV, just above the Piscina level, is a fine mosaic floor, which forms the side entrance, to a semicircular apse, facing south. The chord of the apse has two fluted pink marble columns on it. Both the floor and the walls of the apse were lined with marble. The mosaic is unquestionably Orphic. It is very simple in black design upon a white ground with the usual black line border. The main panel is 6 feet long by 3 feet wide. At the top, or south end, is a bowl with two birds, one on either rim. In the centre is a male head decorated with three-pronged forks of lightning. Beneath this is a boy holding a kid in his right hand. I suggest that the figures are the Kabeiri, Zeus and Pais or the child Dionysius. In a room at the bottom of the steps leading down to Section III, there is another mosaic depicting coloured Gorgon masks. Alongside this room is a large chamber in which were found a statue of Hermes and that of a woman with a cloak, said to be of Sosandra. Judging by the association with Hermes and the proximity to the Oracle, I suggest the possibility that she may represent the Sibyl.

Having reviewed the problem from so many angles, this is a suitable point to follow the story of Aeneas and see how it matches with any of the landmarks in our discoveries. Only in this way, can the full joy of research be appreciated; by bringing to life a story written 2,000 years ago. It is an outstanding tribute to the genius of Vergil, that we and everyone that we have taken down the Oracle, has immediately recognised the Entrance to Tartarus, the River Styx and the Gates of Ivory and of Horn, just as they were described by Vergil.

The *Aeneid* Book VI tells how Aeneas went to consult the Sibyl at Cuma as to how he could visit the Underworld and speak with his father, Anchises. As soon as he landed, he sacrificed to Apollo, and then visited the great temple on the acropolis, where the priests directed him to the Antrum of the Sibyl. Here he made his request.

"Virgin Divine, nothing remains in this life, that can tire me or frighten me. Nothing will be new to me, or that I have not foreseen. I am prepared for every kind of suffering. All I ask of you (since it is here, it is said, that the Entrance to the Underworld and the Lake of Acheron begins), let me come to see my beloved Father. Here is the Gate if you will show me the Road and be my Guide." Thus he prayed encircling the sacred altar with his arms. And the Sibyl replied "Aeneas, Son of Heaven, the way to Hell is easy, day and night the Gates are open wide . . . but to return to see the light of day, that is a difficult problem. To few it is permitted, and only those dear to God, or who approach near to the divine, may come and go like Celestials."

She tells him, that before he will be permitted to enter the Underworld, he must give decent burial to his Steersman, Misenus. Then he must seek out the Grove in the forest where the White Poplars grow, which are sacred to Persephone. There he must find a branch of the Golden Mistletoe, which he must take as an offering to Persephone. From Greek mythology we learn that this was a kind of passport, which guaranteed the return from Hades to the upper world. To help Aeneas find the Grove, his mother Aphrodite sent two turtle doves which flew along, just in front of him and guided him to the tree with the Mistletoe.

But there still remained to celebrate a proper funeral for Misenus. The crew of the ship built a great pyre of oak and poplar logs, with plenty of pine branches to make it blaze. The sides of the pyre were draped with dark green leaves, and they erected round it, a hedge of black cypress. After the body had been washed in warm water and anointed with olive oil, it was "dressed in bright coloured raiment, his favourite gar-

ments". The lament was raised and the body laid upon the pyre. They all took torches, and "averting their faces from the pyre as the ancient rite prescribes, applied the torches to the base." In addition to the body, there had been placed upon the pyre, offerings of food and incense, and bowls of oil. These broke and added to the flames.

When all was consumed, the ashes were extinguished with wine. "Corynaeus collected the bones and placed them in an urn of bronze. He next purified his friends, carrying clean water round them thrice, and sprinkling it in a spray of dew from the bough of a fertile olive tree." The Last Words were spoken and a great barrow built over the ashes. He is still remembered in the name of Capo Miseno, at Bacoli.

Aeneas was then taken by the Sibyl to the Oracle. "There was a deep and rugged cavern, fearful of aspect, from which a poisonous breath streams up from the black jaws of Hades to rise to the vault of sky." Aeneas had already sacrificed seven bullocks and seven sheep at Cuma, now he had to propitiate the Gods of the Nether Regions. "Four black bullocks were the offering to Hecate, Mighty in Heaven and Mighty in Hell, a black lamb to the Mother of the Fates, Dread Night and her Sister, The Earth, finally a barren cow for Persephone. It was now evening, and he began the nocturnal rites to the gods of the Nether Regions, whole carcasses of bulls were laid on the flames of the altar, and anointed with olive oil. After this they entered the cavern. Right at the entrance was a chamber. "In front of the very Entrance Hall, right in the jaws of Hades, Grief and Resentful Care had laid their beds. Shapes, terrible of aspect, have their dwelling there, Pallid Diseases, Old Age, Fear, Hunger, The Counsellor of Evil, Ugly Poverty, Death and Pain. Next is Sleep, who is close kin to Death, and Joy of Sinning, and by the threshold in front, Death's Harbinger, War. And the iron chambers of the Furies are there, and Strife, The Insane, with a bloody ribbon binding her hair." Keith and I believe that these horrible afflictions were depicted on the wall panels of the Painted Room at Baiae.

They went down the Cavern, until they reached the Dividing of the Ways. Here the Sibyl told Aeneas to "Look to the left, where starts the road to Tartarus, there in mud and murk, seethes the Abyss choking forth all its sludge." They reached the banks of the River Styx, and saw Charon "an ancient filthy demon, with ragged white unkempt hair and beard, with a dirty torn garment". He ferries the Shades across the Styx in a leaky coracle made of basketwork covered with skins. "Here all the concourse of souls was hastening to the bank, mothers and strong men, high-hearted heroes whose tasks in this body's life were done, boys, unmarried girls, and young sons laid upon the funeral pyre, before their parents' eyes. The souls stood begging to be the first to make the crossing, and stretched out their arms in longing to the farther shore. But the surly boatman accepted now these and now those, and forced others back, not allowing them to the river side." The Sibyl told Aeneas, that those who have not been properly buried, cannot cross the Styx, but must wait on the bank for a hundred years, before Charon will accept them. Aeneas and the Sibyl crossed over, and on the far landing, found the great three-headed dog Cerberus, who greets all new-comers by wagging his tail and pricking his ears, but is ready to tear in pieces anyone who tries to return to the upper world. "When he growls in all his three throats, the sound echoes through the caverns of Hell."

One day when Keith and I were sitting at the water's edge, we suddenly heard 'Wooooowooooo . . . Wooooowooooo . . . Wooooowooooo . . .' rumbling through the galleries. We were quite sure it was Cerberus, and he had taken a dislike to us. It took several seconds before we realised it was the sound of the Cuma train passing through the tunnel half a mile away. You may smile, but the Oracle of the Dead is a very eerie place, and sitting on the banks of the River Styx two hundred yards underground, is apt to make even the lone bat appear to be the soul of Orpheus still seeking Eurydice in those grim depths.

Soon Aeneas and the Sibyl arrived at the Meadow of Asphodel "where secluded paths and a myrtle wood, hide all those who have suffered and wilted under the harsh cruelties of love." Suddenly, they saw the battlements of the House of Persephone, "and in the archway opposite us the door at which authority commands us to make our offering. Swiftly Aeneas gained the entrance, sprinkled himself with Holy Water, and set the branch of mistletoe upright on the threshold before him."

From this point, the narrative continues as I have related in

L

Chapter II. Aeneas sees his father and learns from him, his future as the Founder of the Latin Race. They then return to daylight by the twin Gates of Sleep, the Gate of Horn and the Gate of Ivory, and go out by the Gate of Ivory. These are the two return passages ending at the Dividing of the Ways.

Having read Chapter IV with the technical account of the tunnels, I am sure the reader will agree that the similarities with Vergil's story as just quoted are far too numerous to be coincidental. Stripped of his poetic imagery, it is a description of a journey into the Oracle complex exactly as we discovered it. For example, the Dividing of the Ways with the smoke pouring out of the 'Entrance to the Tartarus', the River Styx, the House of Persephone with the niches for the Golden Bough, the two gates of Horn and Ivory, and many others all tending to show that this was the centre of Orphic rituals, which had become the most accepted cult in Magna Grecia and among the Italiote tribes by the end of the fifth century B.C. In Vergil's time it aroused great interest among the more cultured Roman youth. It paved the way for the acceptance of Christianity by the Greek world.

Vergil says little about the surface buildings, but this would not be necessary to his poem, so why include it?

The fun of archaeology is making a reconstruction of ancient events. So let me now try to recreate a visit by a suppliant to the Oracle, at a somewhat earlier date than Vergil, say about 300 B.C., before the Oracle became idealised by Orphism. We have quite a number of parallels in the Oracles in Greece, and in the myths to assist us, so the following account is not entirely fanciful. I think the visit of Pausanias to the Oracle of Trophonius, tells us that there, there was an Oracle with very much the same basic attributes as the Oracle of the Dead at Baiae. Here then, is my reconstruction of the visit to The Oracle of the Dead by a Samnite chieftain who wished to talk with his mother recently deceased.

Visits to the Oracle such as that which follows was an event of sufficient rarity to be somewhat of a local sensation. The cost of the ceremonies was considerable. A herd of cattle comprising a couple of bulls, a cow and eleven oxen, together with a little flock of black sheep, was the basic fee demanded by the priests. This would be accompanied by gifts of olive oil, wine and barley cakes, and a bronze tripod for the Sibyl. Accompanied by a retinue of friends the chieftain made his way to the temple at Cuma, paid his fees and made his request. The augurs examined the entrails of the sacrifices. He had paid the correct amount in fees, so the omens were favourable. Accompanied by the Sibyl, he arrives at the Sacred Area at Baiae, where he is met by two young boys who have been appointed to assist in the preliminary rituals. The chief lodges for the night, alone, in the Painted Room. From this moment, all the ritual is directed towards reducing the suppliant into a state of religious ecstasy in which he will believe all he sees and hears during his visit to the Oracle. As he enters the Painted Room, he sees on the walls the horrifying pictures of all the ills man is heir to, Pallid Disease, Old Age, Fear and all those previously catalogued. On the central panel (now erased) there was probably a picture of War, the Harbinger of Death. Just before dawn he is summoned by the boys and taken out to the forecourt. Here he sacrifices a black ewe lamb, and then returns to his lonely vigil in the Painted Room. This regime continues for three days. After each sacrifice the entrails are examined on the marble table by the augur. On the morning of the third day, he sacrifices a black ram. The omens still continue favourable, and at the first signs of sunrise the chieftain baths in the 'D' bath in the east wall of the forecourt. This is the Water of Forgetfulness which had its counterpart at the Oracle of Trophonius. The rest of the morning is spent in fasting and prayer. At noon, he bathes in the 'D' in the south wall, the Water of Memory. It is noticeable that this bath is much smaller than the other. More sacrifices to Hecate and Persephone during the afternoon, then as the sun sets, a black lamb is offered to Night. Now begin the nocturnal sacrifices to the Gods of the Nether Regions. The chieftain is dressed in a white linen tunic reaching to mid-thigh. His hair is bound with white ribbons and he wears sandals on his feet. Around his waist is a belt with a bronze sword.

Now he enters the stair behind the statue niche in the Big 'D' to join the Sibyl in what is now the south tank above. This was formerly a room connected with the north tank and the rear of the temple. It was probably the equivalent of the modern church vestry.

Together they descended the Tholos entrance to the Sudatorium, by a light ladder, placed for the purpose. They then entered the passage and joined the procession in the main Antrum of 270.

There are three entrances to the Antrum. That under the Sudatorium, the Original Entrance, and the trench under the temple. Each one had its role. The Sudatorium entrance was that used by the suppliant and the Sibyl, the priests entered from the temple and the sacrifice from the Original Entrance. In this way, the procession could be formed and all the components fit into their places. The priests dressed in black overalls with pointed headdresses and only slits for the eyes came first. They carried branches of black cypress in their hands. As they passed the Sudatorium the suppliant and the Sibyl took their places behind them. Immediately, the wretched sacrifice followed dragged along by his executioners.

The Sibyl was dressed in scarlet. To the monotonous chanting of the priests the procession went forward. Owing to the narrowness of the tunnel, the suppliant could not turn round and see the sacrifice following, but he could hear its frenzied bleating (or its terrified screams), and feel a nasty cold wind blowing inwards round his legs. Overhead the rolling clouds of black smoke told him they were on their way to Hell. Every few feet there was a flickering smoking oil lamp illuminating the dusty tunnel for a short distance ahead.

They arrived at the Dividing of the Ways. The door to the extension was closed (as it is today), and they commenced to descend the stair of 290 towards the River Styx. As soon as the suppliant had passed, the door was closed behind him. This allowed the sacrifice and its escort to pass directly to the Inner Sanctuary by the South 120. At the same time, the closing of the door must have interrupted the ventilation and filled the head of 290 with smoke from the space now closed by the line of Tiles. Here the Sibyl stops for a moment and says, "Look to the left and note the entrance to Tartarus. It is here that the road to Hades splits into two ways. That on the left goes to Tartarus and that on the right leads on to the House of Persephone, by it we make our journey to Elysium, the other brings evil men to godless Tartarus and with never a pause exacts their punishment." The smoke from 400 lamps and torches all come pouring through this opening into the beginning of 290.

The priests had, probably, also arranged for the doleful voice of Phlegyas, to be heard from Tartarus, "Be warned by my fearful punishment, deal justly with your neighbour and do reverence to God."

They now descended to the Styx, where Charon was waiting with his leaky coracle to ferry them over the water. The Sibyl and he stepped aboard and made the journey to the Far Landing. Here they stepped ashore. Who knows if Cerberus was part of the scene!

They soon mounted the steep stair to the north entrance to the Inner Sanctuary, and as they came round the last semicircular turn in the passage, they entered the ante-room and deposited their offering of mistletoe in the niche outside the Sanctuary entrance.

The Sacrifice was already bound and lying on the altar. By this time the suppliant was almost fainting with fear and religious awe. The priests sat him down beside the altar, with a trench at his feet. He was then told, "draw your sword and be ready to prevent any unwanted Shade from approaching". At this moment he heard a shriek behind and above him, as the High Priest cut the throat of the victim on the altar. The blood poured down into the trench. At this same moment a dreadful moaning was commenced and shadowy faces began to appear on the walls before his terror-stricken eyes. The High Priest called out, "Be ready the next Shade to appear will be your mother." In the state of mind to which he had been reduced, he believed it. He was in fact too terrified to carry out his proposed conversation, and before he could collect his thoughts, the Shade of his 'mother' had disappeared. (This scene would have been quite within the resources of the priests, by means of wooden cut-outs and a lamp to provide the shadows.)

So before he could protest the priests hustled him to his feet and the procession reformed and proceeded to leave the Inner Sanctuary by the 120 passage. At the traverse, the Smoke door was opened to allow them to pass into the South 120, and so to the Dividing of the Ways in a breathable atmosphere. At the Dividing of the Ways, the door was covered with ivory on the west side. It opened to allow the procession to pass. At the same time, it closed the entrance to 290, so there would be nothing to show the suppliant that he was back at the point where he had come in. When the procession reached the passage to the Sudatorium, we think that this was closed by a door and a ladder was standing ready for the ascent through the hole covered by the tile to enter the passage leading to the Room of Memory, behind the temple. Here the suppliant was carefully interrogated, to ensure he believed all that he had seen and heard. If there were the slightest suspicion that he did not accept it, I have not the least doubt, that he would never leave the Room of Memory alive.

We have given a lot of thought to the possible use of the chamber, indicated by the broken walls at the bottom of 290. I have suggested that these may have been the framework for a wooden structure. We think it possible, that where the request to consult the Oracle called for a less elaborate procedure, the Oracle may have been given here. The enquirer was stationed in this chamber, and the Oracle given up in the Rise, the words of the prophesy would echo and rumble through the tunnels, with all the mystery and dread the situation could wish, the Voice of Destiny, the Command of Fate.

I have been in these caverns more than a hundred times and they still inspire me with a certain feeling of awe and dread. The dust from the walls settles on one's clothes, and has a dank smell of death and decay. Even when we get home the smell persists, and reminds us that we have been down to Hell . . . and for this time, we have returned safely.

The ancient sacrifice was not a simple 'burnt offering', it was also the daily meal. In common with all other daily activities, the sacrifice was hedged about with formal religious observances, which were always carefully carried out. The procedure is beautifully told by Homer in the *Odyssey*, when after his return to Ithaca, Odysseus was a guest in the hut of his swineherd Eumaeus.

The worthy swineherd gave a shout to his men "Bring in the best of your hogs," he called, "I want to slaughter it for a guest we have here from abroad . . . And we'll enjoy it ourselves, after the way we have toiled and moiled for the porkers, all this time, with other people living scot free on our work." He then chopped some firewood with his sharp axe, while his men dragged in a fatted five year old hog and brought it up to the hearth. The swineherd, who was a man of sound principles did not forget the Immortals, but began the ritual by throwing the tuft of hair (the forelock) of the victim, into the fire praying all the time to the gods, that the wise Odysseus might soon return to his home. Then he drew himself up, and struck the animal with a billet of oak, he had left unsplit. The hog fell dead. They slit its throat, singed its bristles, and deftly cut the carcase up. The swineherd took a first cut from all the limbs, laid the raw flesh on rich fat, cast the whole into the flames and sprinkled barley meal on top. Then they chopped up the rest of the meat, pierced it with skewers and roasted it thoroughly, and after drawing out the spits, heaped it on platters. And now the swineherd, who had a nice judgement in such matters, stood up, to divide it into portions. He carved and sorted it all out into seven helpings, of which he set aside one with a prayer, for the Nymphs and for Maia's Son, Hermes. He distributed the rest to the company. But he paid Odysseus the compliment, of helping him to the tusker's long chine.

Swineherds were held to be Seers and magicians by the ancients. The Pig was sacred to Demeter. "Then he sacrificed the first cuts to the Everlasting Gods, after making a libation of sparkling wine."

Not all meals were quite like this one, which you and I might have enjoyed. The suitors for the hand of Penelope were waiting for their supper in the palace and . . . "Antinous called out 'Gentlemen, here's a suggestion, we have some goats' paunches roasting there at the fire, which we have stuffed with blood and fat and set aside for our supper'." This, I suppose, was the original 'haggis'.

The setting aside of the portion for the Gods, is still carried out in the towns of Bacoli, Baiae and other towns of Southern Italy to this day. When the butcher kills a beast, he fillets out the Pelvic bone and the hind legs, then hangs this gruesome relic outside his shop, in full view, for the remainder of the day.

The myth of the origin of this practice is also amusing. One day, Prometheus, who was always playing tricks on Zeus, was officiating as butcher and cook at a feast of the Gods. Incidentally, according to one account, Prometheus was the Creator of Man. He fashioned man's image and then one day when Zeus was not looking, he stole a spark from the sacred fire and gave life to the image. When Prometheus cut up the carcase at the feast, he made two piles. In one, the smaller he put all the meat and best fat and covered it with the paunch. In the larger he put all the offal and waste with the bones, and covered it with the hide. Then he called to Zeus to choose whichever pile he preferred. Zeus took the larger pile and then became furious, when he found he had been deceived. He did not blame his own greed. From that day forward, the fat, bones and offal became the portion of the gods. As a punishment for this incident Zeus sent Pandora with her load of troubles to plague mankind which had been created by Prometheus. The worst trouble that she brought was said to be 'Hope', as this causes men to keep on attempting the impossible as long as life lasts. In Greek mythology, Pandora was the first woman and corresponds to Eve.

Apart from this spectacular service, there were many other sides to the work of the Oracle. I have suggested that it was a medical clinic. The hot mineral springs on the floor of the bay offered cures for many kinds of skin diseases, such as eczema and scabies. Also sprains, bruises, and rheumatism would undoubtedly get relief in the warm water.

When the beaches became popular, the business in love potions was very profitable. One can imagine the flighty ladies from the Roman beaches, tripping up to the Sanctuary, for a charm or potion, to attract that goodlooking young charioteer and his friends who drove up and down the Via Herculana in his gold-plated chariot, with the spirited team of four proud horses. Juvenal visited Baiae and noted in one of his satires, the ageing wives who feared to lose their husbands to the young lovelies on the beach, giving such strong love potions that they very often poisoned the poor men.

I have already mentioned the constant demand for omens, by those about to undertake a journey; and the interpretation of dreams, or the giving of spells and counterspells to deal with some enemy. These were all everyday activities of the Sanctuary.

But there must also have been religious propaganda, in the way of torchlight processions after sunset and before the dawn. The nightly sacrifice, again, must have been a wonderful sight. The only light was from the flames of the altar fire. They had music of cymbals, drums and flutes, playing a wild exciting melody. The priests would be careful to observe every detail of the ritual. The ox was led to the altar with its horns gilded and a garland of flowers around its neck, by a group of black robed priests. Now the High Priest robed in scarlet stepped forward and cut the forelock from between the beast's horns, which he threw into the flames. This was done with a sacred bronze sickle. Next, the throat of the animal was cut and the blood caught in a bowl. This blood was sprinkled on the bystanders and the remainder poured into the trench surrounding the altar. The bystanders were then sprinkled with holy water and prayers intoned to the gods of the Infernal Regions. After the usual slices had been dedicated to the gods the rest of the meat was roasted and eaten by all present, in communion with their god, who was represented by the sacrificial animal.

This chapter may contain a great deal that is fanciful, but I hope it has helped to convey an idea of what Baiae may have looked like in those wonderful days. This surely, is the whole object of archaeological research, the enjoyment of recreating the life of the past. I suppose everyone who studies the ancient myths reaches as many different conclusions as those who meditate on religion. Have you ever thought that a church congregation of, say, a hundred persons has perhaps a hundred different ideas of the meaning of the ceremonies. One will think of God as a Father, another as 'A Jealous God and a stern Judge', a child will have one view and a University Don another and so on. It is thus with the myths. Their fascination for me lies in the extraordinary amount of basic truth that can be found in them. Much is even scientific truth, like the story of Orion's dogs which were forgotten in the sea for two months after he was set in the heavens as a constellation. The two stars Sirius and Procyon, the two dogs, lie to the east of Orion and therefore rise above the horizon somewhat later. There are many examples of these poetic explanations for natural fact to be recovered from the myths.

In the account by Pausanias of his visit to the Oracle of Trophonius, we can 'read' quite a lot of extra information into the story, from the names of the characters, and the etymology of some of the words. In his description of the site Pausanias mentions quite a number of deities to whom sacrifice should be made. All these seem to have been former owners of the Oracle. Zeus-Rainmaker was clearly a pre-Hellenic fertility god who had been supplanted by Zeus the King. Hera Charioteer and Demeter surnamed Europa have, at some time, had their surnames exchanged. In Boeotia in pre-Hellenic times there were many shrines dedicated to the Horse Cult of Demeter. On the other hand Europa is always depicted as riding on a Bull, referring to the displacement of the cult of the Earth Goddess Hera by the Bull Zeus. Many of the Oracles that had previously belonged to the Earth Goddess had a serpent as the giver of the Oracle. Then when the delegation went to Delphi to enquire how they should find a means of making it rain, they followed a swarm of bees up the mountain, until it disappeared into the Chasm. In pre-Hellenic days the Mountain Goddess was named Cer, or Q're, the cruel bee-goddess who slew her husband on their nuptial flight. Cer is the same root as the Latin, Cera, 'wax'. Try analysing the myths for yourselves and you will find a delightful new world to explore. I commend for your reading *The Greek Myths* in two volumes by Robert Graves (published by Penguin Classics). Graves has extracted the last possible essence from his examples in a masterly retelling of the ancient tales.

The Oracle was suppressed by Agrippa during the civil war, but I think it would have been allowed to reopen when peace came. How long it then endured, and what functions it fulfilled is almost impossible to decide, or even make an intelligent guess. General indications seem to indicate a decay in line with the world-wide decay in religions which began about 200 B.C. The increasing popularity of Baiae as a Roman seaside resort could not but affect the atmosphere of the Oracle and the Sanctuary. Evidence has been found in Section IV of the ruins that this part of the Thermae was still in use in the fourth century A.D., but there is little evidence to show the state of the rest of the old town during this time.[16] Maybe by the fourth century the Oracle had long since disappeared under the landslide and its very existence forgotten. Pliny the Elder writing when he was admiral at Misenum about A.D. 70 gives a description of this coast in his work *Historia Naturalis*. He says, "and formerly when Puteoli was known as Dichearchia, there was, near by, a City of the Cimmerians". He knew of the Oracle but apparently did not then know of its exact position, or, surely, he would have mentioned such an important site.[17]

It was not until the Renaissance when Vergil began to be read again, that interest revived in the Oracle. But by this time, the view was that the Oracle was an invention of Homer and Vergil. Baiae was just a few jagged walls in the vineyards, no one ever dreamed of archaeological research in those days. So it remained, until Keith and I went in on September 21st, 1962, to solve the mystery of its existence and to add another gem to our inheritance from the past.

I would remind readers that the final interpretation of the use of the Great Antrum at Baiae, will be a matter of close study for the scholar for many years to come. I have only been able to hint at these possibilities in this short volume. I should however like to bring to the reader's notice some fascinating suggestions made by my friend Colin Hardie, Fellow of Magdalen College, Oxford. He says,

I have been coming to a new theory. The disc found at Cuma with "Hera does not allow any further consultation", shows that Hera was displaced by Apollo as owner of the Oracle at Cumae . . . why? . . . and when? Miss Jeffrey dates the disc as circa 500, but Marguerita Guarducci to 575. The temple is late sixth century. Now all this suits the tyrant Aristodemus (of Cumae), and he would have had, like Peisistratus at Athens, a religious policy to do away with all old cults and their aristocratic priestly families and introduced new Pan-Hellenic Cults . . . Apollo at Cumae, and at Baiae the new "Orphic" religion of Southern Italy, Persephina and Dionysius (Peisistratus developed Persephina's Mysteries at Eleusis and Dionysius at Athens). Aristodemus would be likely to start both cults in grand new style and premises, temple and Antrum at Cumae and the same at Baiae. I assume that Ephorus (or Strabo) was right that a king of Cumae suppressed the original Oracle at Avernus perhaps about 650. Aristodemus' grand new cult would have arrived to exploit the Odyssey's Underworld, and its location in the west (Hesiod, *Theogony* 1011-16), making Odysseus father of Latinus, already presupposes the location, but it was built I think to house the elaborate ritual of the Orphic Tablets implied also in the Gold Plates. There is nothing primitive about the Great Antrum at Baiae; it is all of a piece . . . no growth . . . but one grandiose plan as at Cumae.

. . . I incline to think the curious partial blockage is due to the Roman Senatorial Decree *'Consultum de Bacchanalibus'* 186 B.C. (later than Hannibal's visit). The Senate allowed some continuation of cults, if they had a claim to antiquity or to be 'necessary' to a family, because the cult was ancestral, but they might well have forbidden any proselytes or new initiations. In a small way the cult might have continued until Vergil's time, but Vergil was thinking of the original place at Avernus that the King of Cumae suppressed, and Strabo ignores the Baian Cult.

Thus it seems that if, as undoubtedly we should, we give full credence and consideration to the description of the Avernus region given by Ephorus (Strabo) the life of the Great Antrum at Baiae can be roughly divided into three epochs: first the Archaic when it functioned as the Oracle of the Dead, next an Orphic Initiation Centre under Aristodemus, and finally gradually declined after the fall of Cumae to the Oscans and the Romans. When the closure took place is also a problem. In the book I have suggested 37 B.C. as a possible date following the use of the site as a meeting place for illicit cults. Colin Hardie says it may have been following the Senatorial decree in 186 B.C.

All this is but the preliminary to fresh interest in the archaeology of Cuma and Baiae, which our discovery has released.

My story seems to end with a great deal left unsaid. It must be so, with such a colossal subject. Not only have I had to make a selection from the wealth of notes that we made in the field, to condense the story into the limits of one volume, but have had to dismiss entirely the consideration of the many religions that concentrated on the Phlegrean Fields during the early part of the Pax Romana in the first centuries of our era. "All the world was the guest of Puteoli," says one writer who lived there when the Government officials, philosophers and teachers were passing to and fro, bringing with them all the wisdom of the Orient and all its iniquity.

Before closing, I will try and relate what happened at Baiae in the hope that someone will be stimulated to carry on the researches that we have initiated, and so tell of the influence of Baiae on the creation of the Church at Rome.

NOTES

1. The Bible, The Gospel of St. Matthew 2.
2. Homer, *Iliad.*
3. Suetonius, *The Twelve Caesars.*
4. The Bible, The Book of Jonah.
5. Juvenal, *Satires.*
6. M. Pelletini, *The Etruscans.*
7. Herodotus, II, 40-56.
8. Museum at Delphi.
9. Pausanias, VIII, xxviii-xxxi.
10. P. C. Sestieri, *Guide to Paestum,* pp. 29-30.
11. Homer, *Odyssey,* XI.
12. Homer, *Odyssey,* XIII.
13. Homer, *Odyssey,* XI.
14. Pausanias, VIII, 12.
15. Homer, *Odyssey,* XIV.
16. A. Maiuri, *The Phlegrean Fields.*
17. Pliny the Elder, *Historia Naturalis.*

6

Baiae as the Cradle of Italian Christianity

The discovery and identification of the Oracle of the Dead at Baiae, has not only thrown new light on the importance of Baiae itself, but has opened up an entirely new line of research in the Phlegrean Fields.

The transition period from paganism to Christianity, lasted for at least four hundred years. There was no sudden break at A.D. 1. Ever since Baiae had been 'discovered' by the Roman patricians as a desirable seaside resort for the summer season, the region had been growing in social importance. The building of the great imperial palaces and patrician villas, had brought in its train a horde of serfs and slaves of all peoples of the now farflung Empire. Each nationality had its own cult and its own gods, and all of them were worshipped at Baiae in the servants' quarters of the villas and palaces.

For about two centuries before the birth of Christ, as the Roman armies subjugated nation after nation, the local patron gods had lost their power to protect their cities, and their worship had been falling into decline. But man's psychological constitution seems to require a religion for its fulfilment. The Romans were well aware of this, although they were not a religious nation themselves. So much so, that they made the fundamental mistake of offering their deified Caesars to replace the discredited local gods. This merely emphasised the subjected peoples' misery, by a visual witness to their slavery. How could the Romans have expected such a 'god' to offer the consolations of religion to the disillusioned people.

The close contact in the living quarters of the slaves at Baiae created a fertile ground for the dissemination of any religious propaganda that would promise alleviation of their sufferings. It was at this moment that the new teachings, that were eventually to form the basis of Christianity, were being discussed in Syria and Asia Minor, and came to the Phlegrean Fields via the port of Puteoli. Naturally in addition to religious propagandists, all the seditionists, revolutionaries and Fifth Columnists, also came to Baiae seeking support, not only amongst the slaves but amongst the power-seeking Roman politicians also. As early as A.D. 19 Jewish and Egyptian heretical sects were causing trouble by rioting among their compatriots due to their intransigence in proselytising their new creeds. Tacitus tells us that Tiberius had to deal drastically to restore order. "Another discussion (by the Senate) concerned the expulsion of Egyptian and Jewish rites. The Senate decreed that 4,000 ex-slaves tainted with those superstitions should be transported to Sardinia to suppress banditry there. If the unhealthy climate killed them, the loss would be small. The rest, unless they repudiated their unholy practices by a given date, must leave Italy." These were certainly not simple Egyptian or Jewish religious rites as both Judaism and the Egyptian cults were 'permitted religions' and their followers allowed to worship as and where they wished. They were the first exponents of the New Belief to be mentioned by a Roman historian.

When these ideas first came from the east, they were too oriental to suit western ideas. We know from the Acts of the Apostles that St. Paul was a misogynist, and his teachings had no place for women in his religion. But, for a thousand years, the Great Goddess Hera had been adored throughout Magna Grecia. Not only so, but she had been adopted by the Italiote tribes and the Etruscans. The whole local religion was based upon the sanctity of the home and family, with Hera (Juno) as the protectress and patroness. For this reason when St. Paul came in A.D. 59 he had a cool reception by the brethren both at Puteoli and at Rome. Tradition is very loth to change, especially in such fundamental matters as religious aspirations. If you ask anyone, whatever his nationality, or colour, or religion (even an atheist), what are his true religious aspirations you will know he will answer . . . "To live in peace, and family love with my wife and healthy children, to live to see them happily settled in their future life, to have a reasonable share of life's good things, and when I die in the fullness of time, to do so with the promise that in the future life beyond the grave I shall be united with my family."

This was the basis of the religion of the Italiote families, whatever the official hierarchy had to say. It took four hundred years before the early Christian Fathers finally adopted the Great Goddess as the Madonna. Even today this is still a much debated theological question. Every village in Southern Europe has the Madonna enthroned in the Parish Church, yet not one of them, in the minds of the people, is exactly the picture that the Vatican approves. Each of the local patrons is personally associated with the village, by miracles, by having appeared there, or even because she was always worshipped there even in ancient times. To unite this ingrained conception of the need of motherly influence in the home with a religion ruled solely by the male, took nearly four hundred years before a satisfactory compromise was reached. But in Spain, France and Italy, it is still the Madonna to whom the simple people pray.

At Baiae, to add to this confusion, there was a strong Orphic Group, as indicated by the works of Vergil and the finding of the funeral stele at Cuma reserving a part of the necropolis for the use of 'Bacchoi'. When Pozzuoli comes to be excavated, I expect there will be found shrines to all the cults of the Mediterranean area. It was out of this welter of theological disputation that finally the Christian dogmas were formulated.

We can perhaps understand better, why Agrippa found it necessary to suppress some of these cults during the civil war. Agrippa must have relied very much upon the crews of the merchant ships sailing out of Puteoli not only for his officers, but also for his oarsmen. Then in the war against Sextus Pompeius, practically the whole fleet was lost in a storm. This called for complete replacement of the ships and the recruitment of fresh crews. To achieve this 30,000 slaves were freed and trained as oarsmen on the Lake of Lucrino. The timber for the ships was obtained by the violation of the shrines and groves of Apollo inside the crater of Avernus. The Oracle at Baiae had been taken over by Apollo just as the other Oracles had been, even in Greece itself. Maybe, the Mysteries of the ancient Goddess of the Earth were still celebrated at Baiae by the faithful. One can imagine the fury of these at the desecration of their meeting places. Then also amongst the 30,000 freed slaves there must have been many believers in the New Religion, then arising in Asia Minor. These men had made allegiance to a Celestial Power, and they cared nothing for the Roman State. All they wanted was a quick death when they had been promised resurrection and an eternal life of bliss in Paradise. What with these morbid cravings for martyrdom, and the constant bickerings between the exponents of the different cults, the Roman naval staff must have had a very trying time. Things reached such a pass, that even freedom for the slaves was not sufficient bait to join the navy, and those men already enlisted were on the verge of mutiny. There was only one thing to do. The cults of these seditious religions were proscribed and the meeting places razed to the ground.

As we have seen above, it merely had the usual result of driving the movement into secrecy. It flared up in A.D. 19 and again in the reign of Claudius. On this occasion the expulsion of the believers was mentioned in the Acts of the Apostles, as Paul actually lodged with two of them in Athens. Then in A.D. 63 in the reign of Nero there were terrible persecutions in Rome, where tradition says that both Peter and Paul suffered martyrdom about this date.

The campaigns of Octavian leading to his assumption of the imperial throne as Augustus marked the end of the power of the Oracle of the Dead at Baiae. Elsewhere I have suggested that there was a great earthquake which had destroyed the monastery of the Cimmerians which stood in the area upon which Section III was built in the time of Augustus, with its theatre and Piscina at the base of the crater wall. There is still no sign that the Sacred Area was interfered with in any way; it has not been built over. All that was done was to repair existing buildings, as is seen by visual inspection today. It can therefore be inferred that, whatever had happened to the underground complex, the surface buildings were still functioning as a community centre, possibly even as a tourist attraction. We know from Pausanias, and from Vergil, that it was quite the thing to make a tour of foreign lands. Pausanias tells us that at Delphi there were 'guides' to tell the tale.

Whether the Oracle had been transferred to Cuma is a matter of guesswork. It would be quite possible for the priests of the

M

temple there to take advantage of the prevailing disorder to add to their own power by such a course. It is known that the Sibyl continued to be consulted until the fourth century by the Christian Bishop of Rome. Then the whole area was overrun by the Goths. Only recently the International Archaeological Society, excavating a line of shops at the Forum at Liternum about three miles north of Cuma, found a skeleton which had met its death by a blow which fractured its skull, huddled in the corner. Adjacent to this line of shops is a field in which during the last ten years, literally hundreds of Roman coins have been found covering a period from 87 B.C. until the beginning of the fourth century. How did they get buried and scattered over the field in such numbers. I think the explanation was given by the poor victim . . . the town of Liternum was sacked by invaders.

Under the Romans, Baiae became a fashionable seaside resort, and tended more and more to lose its former characteristic atmosphere of gloomy pageantry and mystery. Social activities overwhelmed the pilgrimages to the ancient Sanctuary with wild parties and excesses of all kinds. Tacitus mentions that even the young Caesars used to go out at night seeking the drunks and tossing them in a blanket.

One of the first to build his villa at Misenum was Marius, whose family was one of the leading Campanian country gentry with its seat at Arpinum. He married Julia, the aunt of Julius Caesar, whose family may have been the landed proprietors at Baiae. In any event they had their palace on the southern point of the bay, and Julius Caesar may have been born there. Women make a place fashionable. Both Marius and Julius were ambitious military politicians and their women were helping them with house parties to which all the leading men of Roman society were invited. Caesar's sister was a manhunter. First she married a Spaniard named Lucius Cornelius Balbus who accompanied Pompey when he returned from Cadiz. Balbus introduced the fashion of having troops of flamenco dancers to enliven the dinner parties. There is a letter from the Younger Pliny to his friend Setticius Clarus, who had accepted his invitation to dinner and then not turned up.

How come you accept an invitation to dine and then do not turn up? This is your punishment, you shall pay for the dinner to the last obolus, and expense will not be small. I had prepared a lettuce for each of us, three snails, two eggs, a barley tart with wine mixed with honey cooled in snow (you will pay for this also, as it has all melted away). There were olives, beetroot, marrow, onions and a thousand other things, no less refined. You would have heard an actor, or a poet, or a performer on the lyre, or (judge my magnificence) all three. But you preferred, to partake, in the house of God knows who, of oysters, pickled pork, sea foods and dancers from Cadiz. "You will be punished for your negligence, I don't know how, but surely you will be. You did wrong. You refused a pleasure, if not for you certainly for me, and I hope it would have been for you."

Julia was the grandmother of Octavian, whom Julius adopted as his heir, who later became Augustus. Whilst Caesar was absent at the wars, it was she who entertained the political leaders at Baiae. Then when Julius returned from Egypt in September 47 B.C. accompanied by Cleopatra, the Queen of Egypt and their son Caesarion, the glorious days of Baiae were at their height. Pompey the Great and Mark Antony had villas at Bacoli, and Cicero was the wealthy squire of Lucrino with great commercial interests at Puteoli.

Then in 44 B.C. Caesar was assassinated, and all was changed. Cleopatra must have been at Baiae, when the murder occurred, or it is unlikely she would have been able to escape to Egypt. In any case her ship must have been either at Misenum or Puteoli.

Plus que ça change, plus que c'est la même chose. Crassus bought the villa of Marius and sold it to Lucullus at an enormous profit, but Octavian now ruled in the palace of the Caesars together with his boyhood and lifelong friend Marcus Vipsanius Agrippa. Together they overcame all opposition and Octavian became the Emperor Augustus. A lot has been said in this book about Agrippa, some of which may have given a wrong impression. Agrippa was a very great man. It was he who sacrificed all his own chances to make his friend Augustus the Emperor. Agrippa built the Pantheon in Rome and carried out many other great works including that of surveying the whole Roman Empire. His map was engraved on a marble slab, and was consulted by Strabo when he wrote his 'Geography'. Agrippa was nominated to succeed Augustus as his heir, but unfortunately he predeceased the emperor when he died in A.D. 12. He married Julia, the daughter of Augustus, who was another immoral, or amoral, woman who lived only for personal pleasure. So scandalous did her behaviour become that eventually Augustus was compelled to banish her to the Island of Pandataria.

After the succession of Augustus, many of the former private villas at Bacoli and Baiae had become imperial property. But this only increased the popularity of the resort with the emperor in residence for many months in the year. This was when Horace and Vergil shared "a modest villa" with other poets and writers. They had the friendship of Maecenas who was minister to Augustus. Through him they became close friends of the Emperor himself, who probably spent many hours at their "modest villa" where there must have been a literary circle very similar to that held by Dr. Johnson and his friend Boswell in London eighteen hundred years later.

On the death of Augustus, Tiberius became emperor. He was so fond of the Bay of Naples, that he spent the last nine years of his life, either on the Island of Capri, or in one of the imperial villas at Bacoli or Baiae. We do not know much about Caligula and Baiae, but he was succeeded by Claudius with his notorious Empress Messalina. They spent much time at Baiae. Caligula built a pontoon bridge of boats so that he could visit his friends at Puteoli, whilst Messalina was disporting herself with a long series of lovers on the beaches and at the little theatre, we can still see in the ruins at Baiae. Her fantastic debaucheries included spending nights in a public brothel, and marrying Gaius Silius on the stage of the theatre. For this last excess she was executed by Claudius. Then Claudius remarried, a most unfortunate choice, his niece Agrippina, who was already the mother of the future Emperor Nero. She was a woman who lived for ambition and power. Later when Nero came to the throne, he was already tired of her overbearing dominance and decided to get rid of her. Agrippina had a villa at Lucrino together with some very profitable oyster fisheries which Nero also coveted. Agrippina was accustomed to spend a lot of her time at Lucrino. She poisoned Claudius, her husband, with a dish of poisonous mushrooms in A.D. 54 and Nero was emperor. The story of her murder was related in Chapter I.

Intrigue, murder, cruelty and ambition were the background

to the luxurious front exhibited along the few miles of the shores of the Gulf of Pozzuoli, where for five hundred years the most important men in the whole world had their residences.

Here my story ends. I hope the reader has been able to share with us some of the thrills we experienced when we first entered the great Antrum and made the return journey to Hades in the Footsteps of Orpheus, Odysseus, Hannibal, Vergil and Aeneas, and a legend became History.

Discovery of the Roman Port at Cuma

As this book was going to press, the author announced his discovery of the Roman port at Cuma. This most important addition to our knowledge of the archaeology of the Phlegrean Fields and indeed of the early history of the Roman Empire is another example of success achieved by following the slender clue found in the record by Suetonius of the Sicilian campaign of Octavian. The Roman fleet was completely destroyed in a summer storm, and Octavian was compelled to conclude an armistice with his rival Sextus Pompeius to safeguard the supply of corn to feed Italy. Nevertheless he and his Admiral Agrippa had no intention of accepting defeat. This was in the autumn of 36 B.C. They decided to build a new fleet during the coming winter and to complete it in time for the spring 'sailing season' of 35 B.C. Suetonius tells us that 30,000 freed slaves were to be trained as oarsmen, on the waters of the Portus Julia which they formed by letting the sea into the Lucrine and Avernan Lakes. This number of oarsmen indicates their intention to provide about 200 ships all of which were to be built inside the crater of Avernus, where the new dockyards were established. There remained the problem of supplies and the port to handle them. Misenum was too far away, and the waters of the two Lakes of Portus Julia would be encumbered with the training of the crews and the ships fitting out.

Cuma offered the solution as it was only a mile away. But the Selva Gallinaria, the forest along the sand dune coast was infested with pirates installed there by Pompeius, and there was no port at Cuma. Agrippa faced up to the problem. He cut the Gallery of Cocceius directly from the water level of Lake Avernus to the Acropolis at Cuma, thus providing himself with a safe underground road for his supplies that could not be attacked by the pirates.

There had always been a small fishing port at Cuma situated on an outlet of Lake Fusaro, or Marsh of Acherusia as it was then called. The problem in making a commercial port was to ensure that the entrance would not fill up with sand with every westerly gale. The Phoenicians had solved this many centuries before at their harbour of Sidon in Palestine. Agrippa used their method which was to provide a head of reserve water, that could be released at low tide at the head of the harbour to scour the channel free of sand. This was done by driving a small tunnel through the hill at Torre Gaveta at the southern end of Lake Fusaro. At the sea end of the tunnel a ramp was fashioned about three feet higher than the level of High Water Springs. The breaking seas would run up the ramp topple over into the tunnel and gradually raise the head of water in the lake. At the northern end of the lake Agrippa built a canal to carry the water to a reservoir at the head of his new harbour. This was provided with sluice gates which could be opened after a storm to scour out the sand from the channels. The final touch was to drive a new tunnel through the Acropolis of Cuma so that the stores could be landed at the new harbour and transported on a level road less than a mile long right into the new dockyards at Avernus where they would be needed. This offers the explanation of the reason for the Gallery of Cocceius, which otherwise seems a completely useless expenditure of labour and effort.

The outline of the Roman port can still be seen at Cuma. All the moles, the canal and even the 'lighthouse' (*pharos*) at the sea end of the entrance, the long gut from the *pharos* to the dogleg bend into the inner harbour offer a fascinating page of history that can be read by any sailor. The harbour is large enough to accommodate about a dozen merchant ships with their war-galley escorts, as they arrived in convoy from the northern ports of Cosa, Ostia, Pyrgi, with lead anchors, iron-work, canvas, rope, spars, food for 60,000, bos'un's stores for 200 ships . . . all in the short period of six months in the winter of 36 B.C.

The effort was completely successful. 'D' Day was in the Spring of 35 B.C. when the new fleet sailed to meet Sextus

Pompeius and surprised him off Mylae in Sicily. The battle was fought in rough weather and Octavian was so seasick he could not even rise from his bunk to give the signal to commence hostilities. But Admiral Agrippa was the driving force and victory was soon theirs.

Dr. Paget is still at Baia continuing his researches.

Bibliography

Aeschylus, *Greek Tragedies*, Loeb Classical Library.

The Bible.

Ceram, C. W., *The Secret of the Hittites*, Knopff, New York, 1965.

Clement of Alexandria, *Exhortation to the Greeks*, Loeb Classical Library.

Diodorus Siculus, Loeb Classical Library.

Dionysius of Halicarnassus, Loeb Classical Library.

Euripides, *Plays*, Loeb Classical Library.

Glover, T. M., *Conflicts of Religions in the Early Roman Empire*.

Graves, Robert, *The Greek Myths*, Penguin Classics.

Gunther, A. W., *The Illustrated London News*, Jan. 1964.

Guthrie, W. K. C., *Orpheus and the Greek Religion*, Methuen, London 1952.

Harrison, Jane E., *Prolegomena to the Study of Greek Religion*, Cambridge.

Herodotus, Loeb Classical Library.

Hesiod, *Theogony*, Loeb Classical Library.

Homer, *The Iliad* and *The Odyssey*, Penguin Classics.

Kitto, H., *The Greeks*, Penguin Classics.

Lissner, R., *The Living Past*, Jonathan Cape, London, 1957.

Livy, *History of Rome*, Penguin Classics.

Maiuri, A., *The Phlegrean Fields*, Italian Government.

Moscati, S., *Antiche civilta semitiche*, Feltrini, Milan, 1961.

Pelletini, M., *The Etruscans*, Penguin Classics.

Plato, Loeb Classical Library.

Plutarch, Loeb Classical Library.

Powell-Davies, J. E., *The First Christian* and *Dead Sea Scrolls*, Mentor Books, New York.

Sestieri, P. C., *Paestum*, Italian Government.

Suetonius, *Lives of the Cæsars*, Penguin Classics.

Silius Italicus, *Punica*, Loeb Classical Library.

Tacitus, *Annals of Rome*, Penguin Classics.

Vergil, *Aenid*, Penguin Classics.

Glossary of People and Places

Acheron   A tributary of the River Styx, one of the rivers of Hell.

Acherusia   The marsh into which the rivers of Hell discharged.

Adonis   Syrian fertility god, whose great shrine at Antioch, was known to St. Paul. Adonis had been the god of Canaan for many centuries, being mentioned by Ezekiel. Many of his rites are similar to the Christian. His festival was at Easter.

Aeacus   One of the judges of the Shades in Hades.

Aeneas   Son of Anchises and the goddess Aphrodite. The hero of the *Aeneid*. He was the legendary founder of the Latin race.

Agnano   A crater in the Phlegrean Fields over 5 miles in diameter.

Agrippa, Marcus Vipsanius   Born 63 B.C., was the lifelong friend and genius behind Augustus, the admiral who defeated Pompey and Antony, surveyor of the Roman Empire and builder of the Pantheon in Rome.

Agrippina, The younger   Granddaughter of Agrippa, mother of Nero, murdered by him in her villa at Lucrino A.D. 59.

Anchises   Father of Aeneas, who made the great Orphic speech in the Underworld, when Aeneas visited him.

Anicetus, T. Claudius   A freedman, Admiral of the Fleet at Misenum in A.D. 59 when he murdered Agrippina on the orders of Nero.

Antioch   City in Syria, the centre of Adonis worship.

Antonia   Daughter of the Emperor Claudius, whom Nero put to death for refusing to marry him.

Antonia   Wife of Drusus and mother of the Emperor Caligula, she died about A.D. 36, probably poisoned by Caligula.

Antony, Mark   Born in 83 B.C., friend of Julius Caesar, but enemy of Augustus in the struggle for the succession. Lover of Cleopatra with whom he committed suicide.

Aphrodite   To the Greeks she was the goddess of love and sexual desire, but in Asia Minor she was the Hittite goddess of love and battle. This may account for her being on the Trojan side in the war.

Apis   The Egyptian sacred bull god, later equated with Zeus.

Apollo   God of divination, music, medicine. He took over all the Oracles from the Goddess of the Earth, the principal ones being at Delphi, Delos and Avernus.

Archaemenides   One of Odysseus' crew marooned in Sicily, and found by Aeneas three months later.

Achaeans   Migrants into the mainland of Greece about 1600 B.C. They brought the Olympian Gods and were the 'Greeks' of Homer's 'Iliad'.

Argos   City of the Myceneans in Greece, and centre of the worship of Hera. It was destroyed by the Dorians about 1400 B.C.

Astarte   Syrian goddess, equated with Isis, Ishtar and others. She was the mother of Adonis, and descended to Hades to beg her son's return to Earth.

Athene   Goddess of intelligence and the Roman genius, also of strategy in war. She was said to be the daughter of Zeus, having emerged from his head.

Augustus   Great nephew of Julius Caesar and emperor from 27 B.C. to A.D. 14.

Bacchante   Female dancers and celebrants at the feasts of Dionysius.

Bacchus   Roman name for Dionysius, the God of the Orphics, and famous for his orgiastic festivals.

Bacoli   Roman Bauli, Greek Baoulis, the district between Misenum and Baiae where most of the imperial villas were.

Baiae   Site of the Oracle of the Dead, and the Roman seaside resort in the Phlegrean Fields.

Balbus   A Spaniard from Cadiz, friend of Pompey and Julius Caesar, also of Augustus. Married Caesar's sister.

Bradyseism   A rhythmic rise and fall of the sea level due to volcanic conditions. The period is measured in centuries and the whole of the west coast of Italy is affected.

Calabria   The province forming the toe of Italy.

Campania   Province of Italy that extends from the Gulf of Gaeta to the Gulf of Policastro, and forms a strip bounded on the east by the Apennine mountains.

Capella   Modern village near Misenum, that formerly was the naval barracks of the Roman naval base.

Capua   Known today as Santa Maria di Capua Veteri; was the Etruscan and then the Roman capital of the Campania.

Castello di Baia   Built in the sixteenth century by the Spanish viceroy Don Pedro of Toledo as a part of the defence of Naples. It is said to cover the ruins of Julius Caesar's palace.

Celius, Marcus   Client defended by Cicero on a charge of attempted murder. The speech for the defence gives a vivid picture of the debauchery on the beaches at Baiae.

Cerberus   Three-headed dog in Hades. He was originally the property of Hecate, goddess of Heaven, the Earth and Hell, hence his three heads.

Chalcis   A district of Thrace in Northern Greece.

Charon   Demon ferryman who took the Shades over the Styx in his leaky basketwork coracle covered with skins.

Charybdis   A fabulous monster who dwelt in the Straits of Messina; she personified the tides, and was known to Homer, who tells of her in the *Odyssey*.

Chthonic Gods   These were 'gods of the soil'; the old original gods of neolithic man.

Cicero   Famous Roman politician and advocate who lived at Lucrino. He was born at Arpinum in 106 B.C. and executed in 43 B.C. after the assassination of Caesar. He has left many works that are still read with great interest.

Cimmerians   Priests of the Oracle of the Dead; should not be confused with the Cimmerians who invaded Asia Minor about 1000 B.C.

Circe   An enchantress who entertained Odysseus on his famous voyage. She turned his crew into swine, but Odysseus saved them. Circe told Odysseus how he could reach the City of the Cimmerians, there to consult the Shade of Tereisias in the Underworld.

Claudius   Emperor of Rome, A.D. 41-54.

Cleopatra   Queen of Egypt probably spent four years at Baiae from 48-44 B.C. with Julius Caesar. She escaped from there to Egypt after the assassination where she was joined by Mark Antony.

Cocceius   Roman engineer under Agrippa, who built the tunnel from Cuma to Avernus, and the Crypta Napolitana, connecting Naples with the Phlegrean Fields, under the ridge of the Vomero.

Cocytus   A river of the Infernal Regions.

Cornelius, Cneius   The Roman consul who is reputed to be the first patrician to build his villa at Baiae; 178 B.C. is the date recorded by Livy.

Cuma   For many centuries the chief town of the Bay of Naples area, was captured by the Oscans in 421 B.C. and by the Romans in 334 B.C. Soon after the completion of the Via Domitiana it began to decline; and lose all importance. It was the site of the Oracle of the Sibyl.

Cybele   Great Mother of the gods, an Asiatic deity who was brought to Rome at the command of the Cumaean Sibyl in 209 B.C. Her temple was on the present site of St. Peter's.

Daedalus   Athenian who was the architect of the Labyrinth at Knossos in Crete, was said to be a great inventor, sculptor, architect and comparable with Leonardo da Vinci. He invented the flying machine, sails for ships and may have founded Cuma.

Delphi   Oracle of Apollo and centre of the World. The influence of Delphi on ancient civilisation cannot be over estimated.

Demeter   The corn goddess, known to the Romans as Ceres.

Dichearchia   The Greek name for Puteoli, or modern Pozzuoli.

Diodorus Siculus   Greek historian who wrote in the time of Julius Caesar and Augustus.

Dionysius   Son of Zeus, god of the Orphics, known to the Romans as Bacchus. His worshippers were 'Bacchoi'. His rites are greatly misunderstood when measured by modern standards.

Dioscuri   The twin gods who were gods of horse training, wrestling, and the protectors of shipwrecked mariners.

Domitian   Emperor from A.D. 81-96, built the Via Domitiana.

Dordona   The oldest Oracle in Greece, sacred to Zeus. It had religious alliances with the Oracle at Ammon in Lybia, North Africa.

Drusus   Roman general and grandfather of Caligula. Lived at Bacoli, where his wife kept Moray eels for divining.

Earth (Ge)   The great goddess of the Earth.

Eleusis   City in Greece where the Mysteries of Demeter were performed each September—harvest festivals in fact.

Elpenor   Crew man of Odysseus, who got drunk in the palace of Circe. Fell down a ladder and broke his neck when trying to rejoin his ship.

Elysium   The Land of Joy, the Heaven of the ancients in the Underworld, to be reached by those judged worthy by the Three Judges of the Shades.

Ephorus   A fifth-century B.C. Greek writer whose works are now lost. He was looked upon as very reliable by the other Greek historians, and is often quoted by them.

Eponomeo   Volcano on the Island of Ischia.

Erebus   The deepest and most terrible part of the Greek Hell. The place where the Titans were imprisoned.

Eridanus   A river of the Infernal Regions, where the shades who were about to be reincarnated for a second life on Earth, waited before bathing in the waters of Lethe.

Essenes   A Jewish sect with their monastery near the Dead Sea. Here the first concepts of the dogmas that later became Christianity were formulated during the last two centuries before our era began.

Etruscans   Powerful Italian nation, who prior to the rise of Roman power ruled all Italy as far south as the River Sele. Their origin is disputed. They probably came from Asia Minor, as their art contains much oriental influence.

Eumaeus   The faithful swineherd of Odysseus.

Euripides   Greek playwright, to whom we owe much of our knowledge of Orphism.

Eurydice   The wife of Orpheus.

Eurynomus   A horrible blue-black demon of Hell, who ate all the flesh off the bones.

Falernum   A district of Latium from which came the best wines.

Fusaro   Modern name for the lake which was the marsh of Acherusia.

Gaudo   A neolithic or early bronze age cemetery near Paestum, dating from about 2500 B.C. contemporary with the second city of Troy layer in the hill of Hissarlik on the Dardanelles.

Gorgons   Three nymphs who lived in the area of Lake Tritonis, near the Atlas Mountains. They were so ugly that the sight of their faces could cause death. Gorgon masks were used on Bakers' ovens to scare intruders from opening the door and spoiling the bread.

Hades   Brother of Zeus and lord of the Underworld. Also the name of the Underworld itself.

Hannibal   Carthaginian general who invaded Italy over the Alps, in the Second Punic War. He left Italy in 202 B.C. and was finally defeated at Zama in North Africa.

Helen of Troy   Daughter of Tyndaraeus King of Sparta, wife of Menelaus, stolen by Paris, was the cause of the Trojan War, and the most beautiful woman of her time.

Helius   The Sun.

Hera   Spouse of Zeus, but in reality the ancient great goddess of the Mediterranean region, whose worship the Olympians were unable to suppress. They therefore incorporated her into their Pantheon.

Herculaneum   City on the Bay of Naples, overwhelmed by the eruption of Vesuvius in A.D. 79.

Hercules   In mythology, the son of Zeus and Alcmene. But he is now considered to be a historical personage, probably a chief of Tiryns. He performed the Twelve Labours and then ascended to Olympus to sit at the right hand of Zeus. He gave his name to numerous colonies of early settlers in the Mediterranean area.

Hermes   The conductor of Shades to the Underworld.

Hero   At first a dignity received after death by outstanding terrestial achievements; later it came to mean any son of a god by a nymph or a mortal.

Herodotus   Greek historian, born about 484 B.C., at Halicarnassus', he died about 424 B.C. after writing the long history of Greece and the Persian wars, together with a fine description of the nations of the then known world.

Hesiod   Greek writer and contemporary of Homer. He was the first to give the story of the Creation and the Olympic Gods.

Hesperides   Daughters of Atlas and guardians of the tree which bore the golden apples, in the garden which Ge gave to Hera as a wedding present.

Hestia   Goddess of the hearth and home. She was greatly revered by the Greeks and at public sacrifices she always received the first prayers and libations. The Romans called her Vesta and paid her equal honour.

Homer   Greek writer who lived in Asia Minor about 800 B.C., was the first of the poets. He wrote many works, besides the well

N

known *Iliad* and *Odyssey*. He was held by the Greeks to be the greatest of the poets.

Horace   Roman poet, born 65 B.C. died 8 B.C., lived at Lucrino and was a friend of Augustus, Vergil and many other famous people. He was a great lover of the joys of Baiae.

Icarus   Son of Daedalus, who was killed by his wings melting in the sun whilst trying to escape from the Labyrinth in which he had been imprisoned with his father.

Iris   Messenger of the gods.

Ischia   Island in the Bay of Naples, known to the Greeks as Pithecussae. It was colonised by them about 1000 B.C. The island is dominated by the volcano Eponomeo, which last erupted in 500 B.C.

Isis   An Egyptian goddess, mother of Horus. Her rites and story are similar to that of Adonis and his mother. The worship of Isis was adopted by the Romans. There is a fine temple, extant at Pompeii, which is almost intact.

Julia   Aunt of Julius Caesar and wife of Marius.

Julia   Daughter of Augustus and banished by him for her profligacy.

Julia   Sister of Julius Caesar, wife of Balbus and grandmother of Augustus.

Julius Caesar   Probably born in the palace at Baiae about 102 B.C. One of the greatest military geniuses of all time. Lover of Cleopatra with whom he lived at Baiae for the four years previous to his assassination, in 44 B.C.

Juvenal   The Roman satirist, supposed to have lived from A.D. 50-100.

Kabeiri   Greek gods whose centre of worship was at Thebes in Boeotia; much of their ritual was Orphic.

Knossos   Capital of Minoan Crete, destroyed about 1400 B.C.

Kyme   Greek name for Cuma.

Labyrinth   Home of the Minotaur at Knossos. It may also have been an ancient shrine with a dancing floor in the form of a maze.

Lethe   River of the Underworld, in which those Shades who were about to be reincarnated, bathed to forget their former existence.

Liburna   The light scouting vessel of the Roman navy, said by Pliny to have been copied from the Greek pirate vessels.

Liternum   Town a few miles north of Cuma to which Scipio Africanus retired after his defeat of Hannibal.

Livy   Roman historian born 59 B.C., died A.D. 17. He wrote a great history of Rome from its foundation up to 9 B.C., but most of it is lost.

Lucrino   Modern name for Lacus Lucrinus in the Phlegrean Fields. It was formerly of considerable extent but was almost filled up by the eruption of Monte Nuovo, in 1538.

Lybians   The name given to the first inhabitants of Southern Europe who came from North Africa.

Magna Grecia The name given to the Greek colonies in Italy and Sicily.

Marius Roman general born at Arpinum in 157 B.C. had a villa at Misenum. Was constantly at war with Sulla who finally defeated his son at Nola. Marius died in 87 B.C.

Meadow of Asphodel The first region of the Underworld that the Shade enters after death and before judgement.

Messalina The dissolute Empress of Claudius, who later had her executed for her excesses.

Minos The King, or probably the title of the king, of the Minoans.

Minyad Poem attributed to Homer.

Misenus Steersman of Aeneas who challenged the Tritons to a trumpet-blowing contest. He lost and was drowned as a punishment for his presumption.

Mistletoe The Golden Bough, or passport to Hades which guaranteed a return to Earth.

Mithras Prophet of a religion that originated in Persia. Brought to Europe by the Roman armies it spread rapidly, and for a long time rivalled Christianity. A perfect example of a Mithraic temple exists at Capua.

Monte Barbaro Hills to the north of Lake Lucrino marking its former extension.

Monte Nuovo Volcano 450 feet high that erupted in Lake Lucrino in 1538.

Moray eels These fish were trained to swim in a circle round their tank, bystanders offered titbits to consult them for omens. If the titbit was taken all was well.

Musaeus Son of Orpheus.

Muses Goddesses of the arts and music. There were nine of them.

Mysteries When the Olympic gods came to Greece, the ancient religions were proscribed, but were kept alive in secret by the worshippers and became known as the Mysteries.

Neapolis Modern Naples, probably founded by Samnites, then was a Graeco-Phoenician trading station, settled by colonists from Athens and Chalcis. Under the Romans it became a school through which Greek culture passed to Roman youth.

Nero Emperor from A.D. 54-68.

Octavian Grand-nephew of Julius Caesar who became Augustus.

Odysseus Known to the Romans as Ulysses. His voyage round Italy and Sicily is described by Homer in the *Odyssey*. He is now considered a historic person and lived about 1180 B.C.

Olympic Gods Were brought to Greece by the Achaeans about 1400 B.C. Their coming substituted male supremacy for the ancient matrilineal societies that had prevailed in all areas.

Onomacritus Greek writer of the fifth century B.C. who lived in Athens, he codified the works of Homer and of Orpheus.

Although much criticised for additions and inaccuracies, he did a lot of good work.

Oracles   These were originally chasms in the earth that were shrines of the Earth Goddess, at which divination was practised. They had an immense influence on the evolution of civilisation in the Mediterranean.

Orpheus   The greatest singer and poet who has ever lived. He was said to have founded a way of religious life that would lead to the Elysian Fields.

Osiris   Egyptian god who probably represented the Sun as Isis did the Moon. The myth of the death of their son Horus was the familiar fertility cycle that inspired all the early religions.

Paestum   Greek Poseidonia, a centre of the worship of Hera in Magna Grecia about 60 miles south of Naples. Three of the magnificent temples still survive.

Patroclus   Close friend and companion of Achilles at Troy.

Pausanias   Greek traveller who lived about A.D. 130-180. He wrote a magnificent description of all he saw in Greece, and is a most reliable writer.

Pelasgians   First inhabitants of the mainland of Greece, they probably came from North Africa.

Penelope   Faithful wife of Odysseus, who wove her wedding veil during the day and unravelled it at night to deceive her suitors until his return.

Persephone   Daughter of Demeter and Queen of the Underworld.

Petronius   Organiser of the orgies of Nero, as his equerry. He wrote *Satyricon*, a splendid parody of a feast which is supposed to have been given by Nero at Puteoli.

Phanes   The Orphic creator and ruler of the Universe.

Phlegethon   The flaming river of Hell.

Pindar   Greek writer who lived about 500 B.C.

Pithecussae   Ancient name for the island of Ischia.

Pliny the Elder   Admiral of the Roman fleet at Misenum, during the eruption of Vesuvius in A.D. 79, in which he lost his life in attempting to rescue the victims at Stabiae.

Pliny the Younger   Nephew of above who was at Misenum with him at the time of the eruption. He wrote a thrilling description of it in a letter to his friend, the historian Tacitus.

Polygnotus   Painter of the great picture of the Underworld on the wall of the temple at Delphi, now disappeared.

Pomegranate   The symbol of virgin-birth, also the symbol of death and resurrection.

Pontifex Maximus   The Chief Priest at Rome.

Poseidon   Greek name for the Latin Neptune.

Pozzuoli   Modern name for the Greek town of Dichearchia, and Roman Puteoli, a town in the Phlegrean Fields, that in the time of Augustus was "the greatest port in the world".

Prochida   Prochyta, an island in the Bay of Naples, separated from the mainland by the strait known as the River of Ocean.

Prometheus   According to mythology, he was the creator of man.

Propertius   Roman poet 50-16 B.C.

Punta del'Epitaffio   Northern arm of the Bay of Baia.

Python   Serpent sacred to Hera that was killed by Apollo when he took over the Oracle at Delphi. Zeus decreed that the High Priestess at Delphi should be called 'The Pythoness'.

"Returns"   List of those troops that took part in the siege of Troy.

Rhadamanthus   One of the three judges in Hades. The others were Aeacus and Minos.

Rhodes   Aegean Island that played a great part in mythology.

River of Ocean   (1) The great ocean surrounding the world; (2) the Strait between the island of Prochida and the mainland.

Salerno   Town and gulf commencing at the southern limit of the Sorrento Peninsula and extending southwards for about 100 miles.

Samnites   Numerous tribes akin to the Sabines who inhabited the areas round Vesuvius and the foothills to the east. They founded Pompeii and other towns and were powerful enough to resist the Romans for a long period. They captured Cuma in 421 B.C.

Scylla   A fabulous monster in the Straits of Messina personifying the whirlpools and overfalls. She was known to Homer.

Sele   River in the Gulf of Salerno at the mouth of which the great Heraion was built about 1000 B.C.

Sibyl   The priestess of the Oracle at Cuma. She acted as guide to Aeneas on his journey to the Underworld.

Silius Italicus   Roman writer who wrote about the Punic Wars.

Sirens   Three beautiful singers who attracted sailors to their doom. The story is told in the *Odyssey*. Their location is debated but they were probably near Capri.

Solfatara   Dormant volcano near Pozzuoli. It has not erupted in the memory of man; nevertheless it is only dormant, not extinct.

Sosandra   A statue of this lady is in the ruins at Baiae.

Strabo   Born 63 B.C. died A.D. 21 at Pontus on the Black Sea coast. Came to Rome in his youth and wrote a 'Geography' describing many of the places he visited and many that he did not. He got most of his material from the Library at Alexandria and from the survey of Agrippa in Rome. He is, in the main, a reliable writer.

Styx   A river in the Underworld over which the Shades had to pass to enter Elysium.

Suetonius   Roman writer whose principal work is *The Lives of the Twelve Caesars*.

Syracuse   Chief town of the Greek colonies in Sicily.

Tacitus   Roman historian, A.D. 55-120, friend of Pliny the

Younger, wrote *The Annals of Rome* and several other historical works of great interest.

Tereisias   Thracian Seer consulted by Odysseus in the Underworld.

Teshub   Hittite god equated with Zeus.

Thesprotis   A region of Epirus where there was also an entrance to the Underworld.

Thyrsus   A reed wand tipped with a fir cone and bound with fronds of ivy, carried by the celebrants in the feasts of Dionysius.

Tiberius   Emperor from A.D. 14-37. Spent the last nine years of his life at Capri and Bacoli.

Titans   Rulers of the planets. When the Olympians came they fought the Titans for ten years, then Zeus blasted them with his thunderbolt and threw them into Tartarus where they are to this day.

Troy   City commanding the entrance to the Dardanelles. It was an occupied site from Neolithic times until A.D. 400. There are no less than nine superimposed towns in the Hill of Hissarlik.

Typhon   Lord of the volcanoes whose home is under Eponomeo. His body from the waist down is a mass of twisting fiery serpents; each of the craters in the Phlegrean Fields is a mouth of one of these serpents.

Venafrum   Strabo mentions this region as famous for olives.

Ventatene   One of the Pontine islands used by the Romans (and still), as a prison.

Venus Lucrina   Temple to the goddess is on top of the Punta del'Epitaffio.

Vergil   Roman writer and poet, 70-19 B.C., friend of Augustus and many other important people, wrote the *Aenid* and many fine poems that have survived. He had a great influence on Renaissance authors, and is as popular as ever today.

Vesuvius   The volcano dominating the Bay of Naples. It erupted for the first time in human memory on August 24th, A.D. 79 destroying the countryside for miles around. It has been intermittently eruptive ever since.

Via Appia   Neolithic ridgeway that runs from Rome to Brindisi, via Capua, Naples, Salerno, Taranto. It was later paved by the Romans and named the Via Appia.

Via Campana   Ancient road that leads from Pozzuoli to join the Via Appia about ten miles inland, due north from the town.

Via Domitiana   Built by Domitian, to connect Minturnae with Cuma and Pozzuoli. It shortened the journey to Rome by a day.

Via Herculana   An ancient track, still in use, connecting Cuma with Pompeii, along the coast.

Vomero   The ridge separating Naples from the Phlegrean Fields.

Zagraeus   Ancient god of Crete later equated with Zeus.

Zeus   Ruler of the Olympis Gods and father of mankind.

Zodiac   The belt of constellations along which the sun traces its annual path. It consists of twelve 'signs', each of which originally ruled a month, but owing to the Precession of the Equinoxes there is a displacement over the centuries in an easterly direction, so that today the correspondence with the calendar is very different, from what it was in very early Bronze Age times, or even from 500 B.C.

Index